WISE WORDS

1,001 Truths to Inspire, Enlighten and Enrich Everyday Life

Second Edition

Another Popular ThinkBook™ By
Philip A. Grisolia, CBC

Wise Words

Another Popular ThinkBook™

WISE WORDS
1001 Truths to Inspire, Enlighten and Enrich Everyday Life
(SECOND EDITION)

Copyright © 2009 by Philip A. Grisolia, CBC

ISBN 978-0-578-02204-8

Cover Design By Brian Wilson Visual Communication
www.BWD.bz

Other Popular ThinkBooks™ By Philip A. Grisolia, CBC

101 Questions You MUST Ask Yourself BEFORE You Start Your Business

ISBN 978-1-60743-254-8

30 Money-Making Marketing Secrets No One Every Told You!

ISBN 978-1-60743-254-8

Self-Paced Learning Aids By Philip A. Grisolia, CBC

mindMaster™ Key Phrase Motivators™

ISBN 978-1-61539-134-9

salesMaster™ Sales Stimulators™

ISBN 978-1-61539-135-6

The™ symbol indicates trademarks belonging to Philip A. Grisolia and protected by Federal Law which grants their owner certain exclusive rights not available to any other party or entity.

HOW TO ORDER THIS BOOK:

Please use the Order Form on page 158.
For quantity discount pricing send an email to:
Staff@PhilGrisolia.com.

Library of Congress Control Number: 2009903760

Printed in the United States of America.
Published by Wise Words, P.O. Box 368, Huntley IL 60142-0368
May, 2009

Wise Words

About these Wise Words...

Whether you're buying this book for yourself, or you received it as a gift, this is one of those rare books you're certain to cherish, one you'll enjoy picking up again and again.

By whatever name you choose to describe the *Wise Words* within these pages – truths, proverbs, epigrams, sayings or some other – each of the 1,001 quotations in this book contains its own unique, thought-provoking morsel of wisdom. And, as some wise author once wrote, "...thinking makes us wise, wisdom makes life bearable."

Collecting these *Wise Words* was a joy that spanned more than 50 years. The origins of the wisdom you'll find here extend to the far corners of the world. You may have seen or heard bits or pieces of that wisdom before, but much of it is truly unique, taken from a variety of interesting things I've read, and my conversations with some rather special people over the years, and. As a result, many of the truths contained in this book may be appearing in print for the first time.

The truths you're about to enjoy here are presented in the sincere belief that they have the power to motivate and inspire, as well as entertain you. Yes, many even have the ability to enrich your life and the lives of those near and dear to you.

If you're anything like I am, a good many of these truths will develop their own special meanings for you. For that reason you'll find yourself picking up this book often. Why? Because truth, and the

Wise Words

wisdom it often contains, can do more than merely make life bearable. In the truths you'll discover here there live the seeds of change, change that can give new meaning to your life and the lives of those you love.

That's a rather bold statement, I'll admit, but you'll soon discover that just as with the other 1,001 truths contained in this book that statement, too, nurtures a precious morsel of wisdom.

The people you'll find quoted here come from all walks of life...rich and poor, wise and otherwise, famous and infamous. Included are those who've succeeded in life, and some who are considered failures. Yet there's something to be learned from each.

Some of their names you'll surely recognize, others you may not. But one thing you can be sure of, their motivating words of wisdom – along with frequent glimpses of their wit – span virtually every human experience imaginable.

As you read on, please remember that the occasional use of words such as "man," "he," and "him" in some of the quotations is an indication of nothing more than what it is, a reflection of the times in which those particular quotations originated. In today's world, those truths, like all in this collection, apply equally to women and men.

In the pages that follow you'll also run across a number of quotations that originated with me, either in some of my other writings, or in one of the many college courses I've taught. I doubt you'll call them "profound," but they're certainly worth your consideration.

And, finally, where I was unable to verify the author of a particular quotation, I attribute it to "Anon." for anonymous.

Wise Words

By the way, I did make several attempts at classifying these quotations...by subject, by author, by several other methods. All seemed inappropriate for one reason or another. Therefore, the sequence in which the various truths are presented for you in the following pages represents nothing more significant than the random order in which I carefully selected them from a collection that numbered more than 3,000. As you find favorites among these 1,001 truths, write their numbers on pages 6 or 156 to easily find them again.

Oh, and when it comes to the titles of some of the individuals quoted here – a variety of generals, senators, medical doctors, men and women of the clergy and similar individuals of title or rank – there was no way to accurately determine whether the words attributed to them were spoken before or after they occupied those positions. As a result, most titles have been deliberately omitted.

Having said that, I sincerely hope that your life – like mine – will be motivated and enriched by the knowledge, wisdom and inspiration you'll find in the *Wise Words* that follow.

Phil Grisolia

P.S. If you're curious about the word "ThinkBook™" that appears on the cover of this book, it's a word I created several years ago to describe the types of books I enjoy writing. Those books – including this Second Edition of *Wise Words* – are meant to encourage you and other readers think, to draw your own conclusions about the words I've put on paper, rather than just accepting my ideas. You should always challenge ideas, old ones and new. Question them, massage them, adapt them, so that ultimately you get the greatest value out of each.

Wise Words

**For your convenience, you may write the
numbers of your favorite truths in the space below and on page 156.**

Wise Words

1. There is no future in believing something can't be done. The future is in making it happen.

   Roland C. Baker

2. Ideas are like rabbits. First, you get a couple and learn how to handle them. Soon you have dozens.

   Anon.

3. Not admitting a mistake is a bigger mistake.

   Robert Half

4. Success seems to be largely a matter of hanging on after others have let go.

   William Feather

5. There is nothing like a dream to create the future.

   Victor Hugo

6. Leaders are visionaries with a poorly developed sense of fear and no concept of the odds against them. They make the impossible happen.

   Robert Jarvik

7. Choose a job you love and you will never have to work a day in your life.

   Confucius

8. Do what you can, with what you have, where you are.

   Theodore Roosevelt

Wise Words

9. Leaders are made, they are not born. They are made by hard effort, which is the price all of us must pay to achieve any goal that is worthwhile.
Vince Lombardi

10. You may have to fight a battle more than once to win it.
Margaret Thatcher

11. Success is never final.
Winston Churchill

12. Our business in life is not to get ahead of others, but to get ahead of ourselves -- to break our own records, to outstrip our yesterday by our today.
Stewart B. Johnson

13. The man who goes farthest is generally the one who is willing to do and dare.
Dale Carnegie

14. One of the greatest sources of stress is not being able to complete anything.
Christopher Williams

15. Before following the leader, find out who the leader is.
Dave Weinbaum

16. Watch your thoughts; they become words. Watch your words; they become actions. Watch your actions; they become habits.

Wise Words

Watch your habits; they become character. Watch your character; it becomes your destiny.

Frank Outlaw

17. There is no shame in losing, only in quitting.

Gary Hart

18. Things may come to those who wait, but only the things left by those who hustle.

Abraham Lincoln

19. We must use time as a tool, not as a couch.

John F. Kennedy

20. Go around asking a lot of damn fool questions and taking chances. Only through curiosity can we discover opportunities, and only by gambling are we able to take advantage of them.

Clarence Birdseye

21. Competition brings out the best in products and the worst in people.

David Sarnoff

22. Man cannot discover new oceans unless he has the courage to lose sight of the shore.

Andre Gide

23. Those who say money can't buy happiness don't know how to shop.

Anon.

Wise Words

24. They always say time changes things, but you actually have to change them yourself.

Andy Warhol

25. Opportunity is your most perishable resource.

Philip A. Grisolia

26. If a man doesn't keep pace with his companions, perhaps it is because he hears a different drummer.

Henry David Thoreau

27. You always pass failure on the way to success.

Mickey Rooney

28. Every man who knows how to read has it in his power to magnify, to multiply the ways in which he exists, to make his life full, significant and interesting.

Aldous Huxley

29. Hear reason, or she'll make you feel her.

Benjamin Franklin

30. Determine never to be idle. No person will have occasion to complain of the want of time who never loses any. It is wonderful how much may be done if we are always doing.

Thomas Jefferson

31. A pint of sweat will save a gallon of blood.

George S. Patton, Jr.

Wise Words

32. We must view young people not as empty bottles to be filled, but as candles to be lit.
Robert H. Shaffer

33. Creativity has a lot to do with a willingness to take risks.
Faith Ringgold

34. There are no secrets to success. It is the result of preparation, hard work and learning from failure.
Colin Powell

35. Temper is a valuable possession -- don't lose it.
Anon.

36. Real courage is when you know you're licked before you begin, but you begin anyway and see it through no matter what.
Harper Lee

37. Strange as it may seem, no amount of learning can cure stupidity, and formal education positively fortifies it.
Stephen Vizinczey

38. Work is more fun than fun.
Noel Coward

39. Most people would rather die than think; many do.
Bertrand Russell

Wise Words

40. If I had known then what I know now, I would have made the same mistakes sooner.
Robert Half

41. I look upon life as a gift from God. I did nothing to earn it. Now that the time is coming to give it back, I have no right to complain.
Joyce Cary

42. You can do anything -- but not everything.
David Allen

43. Heroes and winners aren't the same thing.
Michael Kevin Farrell

44. Success seems to be connected with action. Successful people keep moving. They make mistakes, but they don't quit.
Conrad Hilton

45. You can run with the big dogs or just sit on the porch and bark.
Wallace Arnold

46. Success always comes with a price.
Anon.

47. There are three ingredients in the good life: learning, earning and yearning.
Christopher Morley

Wise Words

48. Do the best you can in every task, no matter how unimportant it may seem at the time. No one learns more about a problem than the person at the bottom.
Sandra Day O'Connor

49. Whatever you want to do, do it now. There are only so many tomorrows.
Michael Landon

50. You have to be first, best or different.
Loretta Lynn

51. There's a better way to do it. Find it!
Thomas A. Edison

52. The very essence of leadership is that you have to have a vision. You can't blow an uncertain trumpet.
Theodore Hesburgh

53. The man who removes a mountain begins by carrying away small stones.
Chinese proverb

54. There will come a time when you believe everything is finished. That will be the beginning.
Louis L'Amour

55. Life is like a big baloney sandwich. The more bread you've got, the less baloney you get.
Anon.

Wise Words

56. The minute you settle for less than you deserve, you get even less than you settled for.
Maureen Dowd

57. Every successful enterprise requires three men -- a dreamer, a businessman, and a son-of-a-bitch.
Peter McArthur

58. Talent is only the starting point. You've got to keep working that talent.
Irving Berlin

59. You're less likely to lose too often than to quit too soon.
Dave Weinbaum

60. Doubt is often the beginning of wisdom.
M. Scott Peck

61. A champion team will always beat a team of champions.
Kevin Roberts

62. The life of every man is a diary in which he means to write one story but writes another; and his humblest hour is when he compares the volume as it is with what he vowed to make it.
J.M. Barrie

63. Seventy percent of success in life is showing up.
Woody Allen

Wise Words

64.　Ideas are a dime a dozen. People who put them into action are priceless.
Anon.

65.　Trust your instincts. Your mistakes might as well be your own instead of someone else's.
Billy Wilder

66.　It never fails; everybody who really makes it does it by busting his ass.
Alan Arkin

67.　An extravagance is anything you buy that is of no earthly use to your wife.
Franklin P. Jones

68.　The speed of the leader determines the pace of the pack.
Wayne Lukas

69.　The tragedy of life is not so much what men suffer, but rather what they miss.
Thomas Carlyle

70.　Discontent is the first step in the progress of a man or a nation.
Oscar Wilde

71.　Be patient with everyone, but above all with yourself.
St. Francis de Sales

Wise Words

72. In the long run, men hit only what they aim at.

Henry David Thoreau

73. When one door closes another door opens; but we often look so long and so regretfully upon the closed door that we do not see the ones which open for us.

Alexander Graham Bell

74. A man who says he never had a chance never took a chance.

Anon.

75. There are many bridges to a better life. Knowledge happens to be the most reliable.

Howard Stein

76. There is one thing stronger than all the armies in the world, and that is an idea whose time has come.

Victor Hugo

77. To avoid criticism, do nothing, say nothing, be nothing.

Elbert Hubbard

78. Curiosity is one of the permanent and certain characteristics of a vigorous mind.

Samuel Johnson

79. The real leader has no need to lead. He is content to point the way.

Henry Miller

Wise Words

80. Far better is it to dare mighty things, to win glorious triumphs, even though checkered by failure, than to take rank with those poor spirits who neither enjoy much nor suffer much because they live in the gray twilight that knows not victory nor defeat.

Theodore Roosevelt

81. Insanity is the process of doing the same thing over and over and expecting a different result each time.

Anon.

82. Men do less than they ought, unless they do all that they can.

Thomas Carlyle

83. Do not follow where the path may lead. Go instead where there is no path and leave a trail.

Muriel Strode

84. Common sense is not so common.

Voltaire

85. The man who follows the crowd will usually get no further than the crowd. The man who walks alone is likely to find himself in places no one else has ever been.

Alan Ashley Pitt

86. Everything can be improved.

C.W. Barron

Wise Words

87. If you can't convince them, confuse them.

Harry S. Truman

88. When you arrive at your future, will you blame your past?

Robert Half

89. Good enough never is.

Debbie Fields

90. The impossible is often the untried.

Jim Goodwin

91. We know too much and feel too little, at least too little of those creative emotions from which a good life springs.

Bertrand Russell

92. If a dream comes true just one time, it can change your life for all time.

Anon.

93. The road to success is usually off the beaten path.

Frank Tyger

94. The first man gets the oyster, the second man gets the shell.

Andrew Carnegie

95. Shallow men believe in luck -- wise men in cause and effect.

Ralph Waldo Emerson

Wise Words

96. The great art of governing consists of not letting men grow old in their jobs.
Napoleon Bonaparte

97. The dread of doing a task uses up more time and energy than doing the task itself.
Rita Emmett

98. Genius is the gold in the mine; talent is the miner who works and brings it out.
Marguerite Blessington

99. Success is the child of audacity.
Benjamin Disraeli

100. These things are good in small measure but evil in large: yeast, salt and hesitation.
The Talmud

101. Excuses are the nails used to build a house of failure.
Anon.

102. Anyone can hold the helm when the sea is calm.
Publilius Syrus

103. Lost yesterday, somewhere between sunrise and sunset, two golden hours, each with sixty diamond minutes. No reward is offered for they are gone forever.
Horace Mann

Wise Words

104. Failure doesn't kill you, it increases your desire to make something happen.

Kevin Costner

105. Daring ideas are like chessmen moved forward; they may be beaten, but they may also start a winning game.

Goethe

106. You will only succeed if you know what you are doing is right, and you know how to bring out the best in people.

Margaret Thatcher

107. The world has the habit of making room for the man whose words and actions show that he knows where he is going.

Napoleon Hill

108. Beware of the man who urges an action in which he himself incurs no risk.

Joaquin Setani

109. Money never starts an idea. It is always the idea that starts the money.

Owen Laughlin

110. A ship in a harbor is safe, but that is not what ships are built for.

John A. Shedd

111. Only an inventor knows how to borrow, and every man is or should be an inventor.

Ralph Waldo Emerson

Wise Words

112.   Success is getting what you want; happiness is wanting what you get.
Anon.

113.   A man's dream should always exceed his reach.
Donald Thornton

114.   The shrimp that falls asleep is swept away by the current.
Spanish proverb

115.   Half of our mistakes in life arise from feeling when we ought to think, and thinking when we ought to feel.
John Collins

116.   Bureaucracy is the death of any achievement.
Albert Einstein

117.   You get older, and sometimes it's a chore to hang on to your optimism.
Ron Howard

118.   Life is often compared to a marathon, but I think it is more like being a sprinter: long stretches of hard work punctuated by brief moments in which we are given the opportunity to perform at our best.
Michael Johnson

119.   It takes a lot of things to prove you are smart, but only one thing to prove you are ignorant.
Don Herold

Wise Words

120. Accept the challenges so that you may feel the exhilaration of victory.
                                            George S. Patton, Jr.

121. Our aspirations are our possibilities.
                                            Robert Browning

122. It's okay not to know what you want to do. The idea of trying everything is important. Your experiences come together and make you multi-dimensional.
                                            Jill Elikann Barad

123. Time is a great teacher, but unfortunately it kills all its pupils.
                                            Hector Berloiz

124. The man who does not read good books has no advantage over the man who can't read them.
                                            Mark Twain

125. Adventure is worthwhile in itself.
                                            Amelia Earhart

126. The life force is vigorous. The delight that accompanies it counter balances all the pains and hardships that confront men.
                                            Somerset Maugham

127. If you always feed your mind the same food, how will your brain get nourished.
                                            Becky Roloff

Wise Words

128. In every affair consider what precedes and what follows. Then undertake it.
Epictitus

129. Any fool can criticize, condemn and complain -- and most of them do.
Dale Carnegie

130. There is the risk you cannot afford to take, and then there is the risk you cannot afford not to take.
Peter F. Drucker

131. Experience is not what happens to you. It is what you do with what happens to you.
Aldous Huxley

132. The tragedy of life is what dies within a man while he still lives.
Albert Schweitzer

133. What is vision? It is a compelling image of an achievable future.
Laura Berman Fortgang

134. Make it a point to do something every day that you don't want to do. This is the golden rule for acquiring the habit of doing your duty without pain.
Mark Twain

135. A leader is a dealer in hope.
Napoleon Bonaparte

Wise Words

136. Every man takes the limits of his own field of vision for the limits of the world.

                            Arthur Schopenhauer

137. Success is not permanent. The same is also true of failure.

                            Anon.

138. Worry is interest paid on trouble before it falls due.

                            William Inge

139. Even if you're on the right track, you'll get run over if you just sit there.

                            Will Rogers

140. Time is an equal opportunity employer. Each human being has exactly the same number of hours and minutes every day. Rich people can't buy time. Scientists can't invent new minutes. And you can't save time to spend on another day. Even so, time is amazingly fair and forgiving. No matter how much time you've wasted in the past, you still have an entire tomorrow. Success depends upon using time wisely -- by planning and setting priorities. Time is worth more than money. By killing time, we kill our own chances for success.

                            Dennis Waitley

141. How fantastic is an unexpected victory.

                            Dave Weinbaum

Wise Words

142. The future has waited long enough; if we do not grasp it, other hands, grasping hard and bloody, will.

Adlai Stevenson

143. Good things come to those who wait, but great things come to those who hustle.

Corky Purcell

144. If you don't risk anything, you risk even more.

Erica Jong

145. A man can succeed at anything -- it is all a matter of will.

Elbert Hubbard

146. Too many people overvalue what they are not and undervalue what they are.

Malcolm S. Forbes

147. If you're having difficulty coming up with new ideas, then slow down.

Natalie Goldberg

148. People who believe a problem can be solved tend to get busy solving it.

William Raspberry

149. Strength is a matter of the made-up mind.

John Beecher

Wise Words

150. If we had no winter, the spring would not be so pleasant; if we did not sometimes taste of adversity, prosperity would not be so welcome.

Anne Bradstreet

151. The pessimist sees the difficulty in every opportunity; the optimist the opportunity in every difficulty.

L.P. Jacks

152. Everything is impossible until somebody does it.

Charles Osgood

153. The quality of a person's life is in direct proportion to their commitment to excellence, regardless of their chosen field of endeavor.

Vince Lombardi

154. If you act in usual ways, you won't get anywhere.

Henri Termeer

155. Some folks want their luck buttered.

Thomas Hardy

156. Admit your errors before someone else exaggerates them.

Andrew V. Mason

157. There is more dynamite in an idea than in many bombs.

John H. Vincent

Wise Words

158. If you have built castles in the air, your work need not be lost; that is where they should be. Now put foundations under them.

Henry David Thoreau

159. It is how one deals with setbacks and disappointments that ultimately determines success.

R.C. Archibald

160. The essential factor that lifts one man above his fellows in terms of achievement and success is his capacity for greater self-discipline.

Ray Kroc

161. Failure is an event, not a person.

William D. Brown

162. Martyrdom is the only way in which a man can become famous without ability.

George Bernard Shaw

163. Choice not chance determines destiny.

Anon.

164. Whatever your life's work, do it well. A man should do his job so well that the living, the dead, and the unborn could not to it better.

Martin Luther King, Jr.

165. Knowledge comes, but wisdom lingers.

Alfred Lord Tennyson

Wise Words

166. If you can actually count your money, you are not a rich man.

                                J. Paul Getty

167. Discoveries are often made by not following instructions, by going off the main road, by trying the untried.

                                Frank Tyger

168. Lead with ideas and people will follow.

                                Anon.

169. Money is what people without talent use to keep score.

                                Jeremy C. Epworth

170. No one has the divine right to survive and to prosper. It is a right that must be earned day in and day out.

                                John Stewart Mill

171. When face to face with oneself, there is no cop-out.

                                Duke Ellington

172. From everything you attempt, you learn something new, different or exciting. When you attempt nothing, you have chosen to remain stagnant in a world that is constantly changing, chosen to remain what you are rather than discover what you can become.

                                Philip A. Grisolia

173. Nothing comes to those who wait.

                                Anon.

Wise Words

174. To accomplish great things, we must not only act, but also dream; not only plan, but also believe.
Anatole France

175. Cultivate only the habits you are willing to have master you.
Elbert Hubbard

176. Nothing astonishes men so much as common-sense.
Ralph Waldo Emerson

177. He who hesitates is a damn fool.
Mae West

178. Opportunities are usually disguised as hard work, so most people don't recognize them.
Ann Landers

179. Research is what I'm doing when I don't know what I'm doing.
Wernher von Braun

180. Most people would succeed in small things if they were not troubled with great ambitions.
Longfellow

181. Hide from risk and you hide from its rewards.
Anon.

182. You can be young without money, but you can't be old without it.
Tennessee Williams

Wise Words

183. Don't tell me how hard you work; tell me how much you get done.
James Ling

184. The man who can make hard things easy is the educator.
Ralph Waldo Emerson

185. Money is a terrible master, but an excellent servant.
P.T. Barnum

186. You don't stop laughing because you grow old, you grow old because you stopped laughing.
Anon.

187. Time is your most fleeting resource.
Philip A. Grisolia

188. You have to be open to the unexpected so that if you come upon a discovery you'll recognize it and act upon it.
Stephanie Kwolek

189. Creativity gets stifled when everyone has to follow the rules.
David M. Kelley

190. If you have a job without aggravations, you don't have a job.
Malcomb S. Forbes

Wise Words

191. Good judgement comes from experience, and experience comes from bad judgment.
Randas Jose Vilela Batista

192. He who lives upon hope will die fasting.
Benjamin Franklin

193. If you let failure bother you, you'll never succeed.
John Peterman

194. The Golden Rule: Whoever has the gold makes the rules.
Anon.

195. A man who wants to lead the orchestra must turn his back on the crowd.
Max Lucado

196. Work is love made visible.
Kahlil Gibran

197. Elephants suffer from too much patience. Their exhibitions of it may seem superb -- such power and such restraint, combined, are noble -- but a quality carried to excess defeats itself.
Clarence Day

198. Success is found in much smaller portions than most people realize.
Michael Johnson

Wise Words

199. Creativity is allowing yourself to make mistakes. Art is knowing which ones to keep.
        Scott Adams

200. There's always something to suggest that you'll never be who you wanted to be. Your choice is to take it or keep on moving.
        Phylicia Rashad

201. If you make people think they're thinking, they'll love you; but if you really make them think they'll hate you.
        Don Marquis

202. Experience is a good teacher, but her fees are very high.
        William Inge

203. Prosperity is only an instrument to be used, not a deity to be worshipped.
        Calvin Coolidge

204. Knowledge is the frontier of tomorrow.
        Dennis Waitley

205. There is time enough for everything in the course of the day if you do but one thing at once; but there is not time enough in the year if you will do two things at a time.
        Lord Chesterfield

206. The greatest pleasure in life is accomplishing what people say can't be done.
        Philip A. Grisolia

Wise Words

207. The beginning is the most important part of work.

Plato

208. I don't want a lawyer to tell me what I cannot do; I hire him to tell me how to do what I want to do.

J.P. Morgan

209. Reason guides but a small part of man, the least interesting part. The rest obeys feeling, true or false, and passion, good or bad.

Joseph Roux

210. Success is 99 percent failure.

Soichiro Honda

211. The secret of getting ahead is getting started. The secret of getting started is breaking your complex, overwhelming tasks into manageable tasks, and then starting on the first one.

Mark Twain

212. Most people seek after what they do not possess and are enslaved by the very things they want to acquire.

Anwar Sadat

213. Virtually every important action in life involves educated guesswork. Too few chances reliably translate into too few victories.

Thomas W. Hazlett

214. You cannot create experience. You must undergo it.

Albert Camus

Wise Words

215. Do not spoil what you have by desiring what you do not, for what you now have was once among the things you only hoped for.
Epicures

216. Great works are performed by perseverance, not strength.
Samuel Johnson

217. If you don't do your own thinking, someone else will do it for you.
Edward De Bono

218. The highest reward for a man's toil is not what he gets for it, but what he becomes by it.
John Ruskin

219. Change is certain.
E.H. Carr

220. To achieve the marvelous, it is precisely the unthinkable that must be thought.
Tom Robbins

221. Bravery is the capacity to perform properly even when scared half to death.
Omar M. Bradley

222. While it's important to win, it's imperative to compete.
Dave Weinbaum

223. The two most common elements in the world are hydrogen and stupidity.
Anon.

Wise Words

224. No day in which you learn something is a complete loss.

David Eddings

225. I'd rather try and fail than not try at all.

Stephen Flood

226. One of the greatest discoveries man makes, one of his great surprises, is to find he can do what he was afraid he couldn't do. Most of the bars we beat against are in ourselves -- we put them there, and we can take them down.

Henry Ford

227. Experience is the name we give our mistakes.

Oscar Wilde

228. Persistence is what makes the impossible possible, the possible likely, and the likely definite.

Robert Half

229. We write our own destiny; we become what we do.

Mme. Chiang Kai-shek

230. The trouble with being poor is that it takes up all your time.

William De Kooning

231. If you don't know where you're going, when you get there you'll be lost.

Yogi Berra

Wise Words

232. Plans will get you into things, but you have got to work your way out.
Will Rogers

233. The more I want to get something done, the less I call it work.
Richard Bach

234. Entrepreneurs must learn to bleed. It keeps them alert. After all, failures are but learning experiences.
Wilson L. Harrell

235. Procrastination is like a credit card; it's lots of fun until you get the bill.
Christopher Parker

236. The best way to predict the future is to create it.
Peter F. Drucker

237. In order to become a hero, it's important to survive.
Rommel

238. Being a woman is a terribly difficult task since it consists principally in dealing with men.
Joseph Conrad

239. It's a recession when your neighbor loses his job; it's a depression when you lose yours.
Harry Truman.

Wise Words

240. Creativity comes from having an inquisitive mind, from being easily bored, from wanting to challenge the status quo.

Twyla Tharp

241. What the wise do in the beginning, fools do in the end.

Warren Buffett

242. Every great mistake has a halfway moment, a split-second when it can be recalled and perhaps remedied.

Pearl S. Buck

243. Recovering from failure is often easier than building from success.

Michael D. Eisner

244. Why do I work? I work for just the pleasure I find in work, the satisfaction there is in developing things, in creating. The person who does not work for the love of work, but only for money, is not likely to make money, nor to find much fun in life.

Charles M. Schwab

245. We do experience moments absolutely free from worry. These brief respites are called panic.

Cullen Hightower

246. Organizing is what you do before you do something so that when you do it it's not all mixed up.

A.A. Miline

37

Wise Words

247. Motivation gets you started. Habit keeps you going.
Jim Ryan

248. We learn from experience that we don't ever learn from experience.
George Bernard Shaw

249. If you turn the imagination loose like a hunting dog, it will often return with the bird in its mouth.
William Maxwell

250. Good ideas come when people with different perspectives work together on the same problem.
Mary Ellen Heyde

251. Action is the antidote to despair.
Joan Baez

252. Paying attention to simple things most men neglect makes a few men rich.
Henry Ford

253. Be incredibly curious and seek to learn why and why not, not just whether or not.
Anon.

254. Men can do jointly what they cannot do singly; their union of minds and hands, that focus of power, becomes almost omnipotent.
Daniel Webster

255. You've got to take the bull by the teeth.
Sam Goldwyn

Wise Words

256. I never did anything worth doing by accident, nor did any of my inventions come by accident; they came by work.

Thomas A. Edison

257. Avoid having your ego so close to your position that when your position falls, your ego goes with it.

Colin Powell

258. The man who wins may have been counted out several times, but he didn't hear the referee.

H.E. Dansen

259. No age or time of life, no position or circumstance, has a monopoly on success. Any age is the right age to start doing!

Gerard

260. The past, the present and the future are really one -- they are today.

Stowe

261. It is the growling man who lives a dog's life.

Coleman Cox

262. Great opportunities are often fleeting.

Anon.

263. Happiness doesn't come from doing what we like to do, but from liking what we have to do.

Wilfred Peterson

Wise Words

264. There is no fate that plans men's lives. Whatever comes to us, good or bad, is usually the result of our own action or lack of action.
Herbert N. Casson

265. All things are possible to him that believeth.
Mark 9:23

266. Enthusiasm is the greatest asset in the world. It beats money, power and influence.
Henry Chester

267. Things and people not actively in use age twice as fast.
Arnold Bennett

268. Marriage is our last best chance to grow up.
Joseph Barth

269. Imagination is more important than knowledge.
Albert Einstein

270. Mistakes are a fact of life. It is how you respond that counts.
Nikki Giovanni

271. It is not whether you get knocked down. It's whether you get up again.
Vince Lombardi

Wise Words

272. Ignorance is not innocence but sin.

> **Robert Browning**

273. Our bodies are where we stay; our souls are what we are.

> **Cecil Baxter**

274. Capitalism is what people do if you leave them alone.

> **Swraj Paul**

275. I am only one, but I am still one. I cannot do everything, but still I can do something. I will not refuse to do the something I can do.

> **Helen Keller**

276. No matter what accomplishments you achieve, somebody helped you.

> **Althea Gibson**

277. Imagination is the highest kite that one can fly.

> **Lauren Bacall**

278. The obvious stupidity of ideas seldom impede their progress.

> **Anon.**

279. Trust yourself. You know more than you think you do.

> **Benjamin Spock**

280. Curiosity will conquer fear even more than bravery will.

> **James Stephens**

Wise Words

281. I don't believe in pessimism. If something doesn't come up the way you want, forge ahead. If you think it's going to rain, it will.
Clint Eastwood

282. Sometimes it takes a step backward to remind you what's required to move ahead.
Anon.

283. If you wait, all that happens is that you get older.
Larry McMurtry

284. You take all the experience and judgment of men over 50 out of the world and there wouldn't be enough left to run it.
Henry Ford

285. Success is a journey, not a destination.
Ben Sweetland

286. The supreme accomplishment is to blur the line between work and play.
Arnold Toynbee

287. The time to relax is when you don't have time for it.
Sydney J. Harris

288. The value of knowledge far surpasses the cost of its acquisition.
Anon.

Wise Words

289. A stumble may prevent a fall.

English proverb

290. One of the illusions of life is that the present hour is not the critical, decisive hour. Write in your heart that every day is the best day of the year.

Ralph Waldo Emerson

291. A well-defined problem is half solved.

Ken Morris

292. Always do right. This will satisfy some people and astonish the rest.

Mark Twain

293. A search for someone to blame is always successful.

Robert Half

294. To be upset over what you don't have is to waste what you do have.

Ken S. Keyes, Jr.

295. A bad situation that drifts away always gets worse.

Felix Rohatyn

296. Fall seven times, stand up eight.

Japanese proverb

Wise Words

297. Ideas are like wandering sons. They show up when you least expect them.
Ben Williams

298. You have to be obsessed with an idea to succeed. It must drive you, instead of you driving it.
Christine Valmy

299. All truly great thoughts are conceived while walking.
Friedrich Nietzsche

300. Power is the greatest aphrodisiac.
Henry A. Kissinger

301. Sometimes you have to look reality in the eye and deny it.
Garrison Keillor

302. Life is easier to bear than you think. All that is necessary is to accept the impossible, do without the indispensable and bear the intolerable.
Kathleen Norris

303. Ignorance is not bliss, it is oblivion.
Philip Wylie

304. The will to win is not nearly as important as the will to prepare to win.
Bobby Knight

Wise Words

305. Opportunity is often difficult to recognize; we usually expect it to beckon us with beepers and billboards.

William A. Ward

306. Forget the past. No one becomes successful in the past.

Anon.

307. Success without honor is an unseasoned dish; it will satisfy your hunger, but it won't taste good.

Joe Paterno

308. He turns not back who is bound to a star.

Leonardo da Vinci

309. What I still ask for daily is for life as long as I have work to do, and work as long as I have life.

Reynolds Price

310. Preconceived notions are the locks on the door of wisdom.

Merry Browne

311. Wisdom is the quality that keeps you from getting into situations where you need it.

Doug Larson

312. Optimism is an intellectual choice.

Diana Schneider

Wise Words

313. **W**hen wealth is lost, nothing is lost; when health is lost, something is lost; when character is lost, all is lost.
German proverb

314. **N**ever be afraid to sit a while and think.
Lorraine Hansberry

315. **N**othing is too small to know, and nothing too big to attempt.
William Van Horne

316. **W**e don't know where we are until we see what we can do.
Martha Grimes

317. **I** never worry about action, but only about inaction.
Winston Churchill

318. **W**ork keeps us from three evils: boredom, vice and need.
Voltaire

319. **I** couldn't wait for success, so I went ahead without it.
Jonathan Winters

320. **M**any of life's failures are people who did not realize how close they were to success when they gave up.
Thomas A. Edison

321. **Y**ou're never a loser until you quit trying.
Mike Ditka

Wise Words

322. The brilliant moves we occasionally make would not be possible without the prior dumb ones.
Stanley Goldstein

323. In the ability to deceive oneself is great talent shown.
Anatole France

324. The best discipline, maybe the only discipline that really works, is self-discipline.
Walter Kiechel III

325. The way to secure success is to be more anxious about obtaining it than about deserving it.
William Hazlitt

326. Throughout history the most common debilitating human ailment has been cold feet.
Anon.

327. The secret point of money and power in America is neither the things that money can buy, nor power for power's sake, but absolute personal freedom, mobility and privacy.
Joan Didion

328. A committee can make a decision that is dumber than any of its members.
David B. Coblitz

329. A fellow doesn't last long on what he has done. He has to keep on delivering.
Carl Hubbell

Wise Words

330. Learning time is not a respected part of a work environment. But don't be so busy that you allow yourself to get stupid.

Anon.

331. You can have it all. You just can't have it all at once.

Oprah Winfrey

332. If you can't excel with talent, triumph with effort.

Dave Weinbaum

333. Ability has nothing to do with opportunity.

Napoleon Bonaparte

334. There are two things to aim at in life: first, to get what you want, after that to enjoy it. Only the wisest of men achieve the second.

Logan P. Smith

335. Every spirit makes its house, but as afterwards the house confines the spirit, you had better build well.

Elbert Hubbard

336. The first and worst of all frauds is to cheat oneself.

Gamaliel Bailey

337. We learn from our mistakes, and the amount we learn is in direct proportion to the amount we suffer from having made them.

Tommy Prothro

Wise Words

338. The best executive is the one who has sense enough to pick good men to do what he wants done, and self-restraint enough to keep from meddling with them while they do it.

Theodore Roosevelt

339. Predictability can lead to failure.

T. Boone Pickens

340. Those who make their jobs important often find their jobs do the same for them.

Anon.

341. What we do not understand, we do not possess.

Goethe

342. The more original a discovery, the more obvious it seems afterward.

Arthur Koestler

343. If a man had as many ideas during the day as he does when he has insomnia, he'd make a fortune.

Griff Niblack

344. Never bid the devil good morning 'til you meet him.

William A. Redmond

345. Achievement is largely the product of steadily raising one's levels of aspiration and expectation.

Jack Nicklaus

Wise Words

346. The employer generally gets the employee he deserves.

Sir Walter Bilbey

347. If we listen to our intellect, we'd never have a love affair. We'd never have a friendship. We'd never go into business, because we'd be cynical. Well, that's nonsense. You've got to jump off cliffs all the time and build your wings on the way down.

Ray Bradbury

348. We live by encouragement and die without it -- slowly, sadly, angrily.

Celeste Holm

349. The great thing in this world is not so much where we stand but in what direction we are moving.

Oliver Wendell Holmes, Sr.

350. Trust in God and do something.

Mary Lyon

351. Ability will never catch up with the demand for it.

Malcolm S. Forbes

352. The two common reasons for losing are not knowing you're competing in the first place, and not knowing with whom you really are competing.

Philip Simborg

Wise Words

353. In the business world, everyone is paid in two coins, cash and experience. Take the experience first. The cash will come later.
Harold Green

354. Wisdom oftentimes consists of knowing what to do next.
Herbert Hoover

355. Time, for all its smuggling in of new problems, conspicuously cancels others.
Clara Winston

356. People want to know how much you care before they care how much you know.
James F. Hind

357. High expectations are the key to everything.
Sam Walton

358. People would rather be pleasantly surprised than bitterly disappointed.
Anon.

359. The success of each is dependent upon the success of the other.
John D. Rockefeller, Jr.

360. The man who is waiting for something to turn up might start on his shirt sleeves.
Garth Henrichs

Wise Words

361. God is not a cosmic bell-boy for whom we can press a button to get things.

Henry Emerson Fosdick

362. In Japan we have the phrase, "shoshin," which means "beginner's mind." Our "original mind" includes everything within itself. It is always rich and sufficient within itself. This does not mean a closed mind, but actually an empty mind and a ready mind. If your mind is empty, it is always ready for anything. It is open to everything. In the beginner's mind, there are many possibilities. In the expert's mind there are few.

Shunyu Suzuki

363. There must always be some who are brighter and some who are stupider. The latter make up for it by being better workers.

Bertolt Brecht

364. The reward for work well done is the opportunity to do more.

Jonas Salk

365. Talent is a flame. Genius is a fire.

Ben Williams

366. Look at a day when you are supremely satisfied at the end. It's not a day when you lounge around doing nothing. It's when you've had everything to do, and you've done it.

Margaret Thatcher

Wise Words

367. Life is half spent before one knows what it is.

French proverb

368. Everything looks impossible for the people who never try anything.

Jean-Louis Etienne

369. We act as though comfort and luxury were the chief requirements in life, when all that we need to make us really happy is something to be enthusiastic about.

Charles Kingley

370. Even Noah got no salary for the first six months -- partly on account of the weather, and partly because he was learning navigation.

Mark Twain

371. Money is like a sixth sense...you need it to appreciate the other five.

Somerset Maugham

372. There is nothing wrong with men possessing riches. The wrong comes when riches possess men.

Billy Graham

373. There is no security on this earth; there is only opportunity.

Douglas MacArthur

374. To tend unfailingly, unflinchingly toward a goal is the secret of success.

Anna Pavlova

Wise Words

375. He who would govern others should first be the master of himself.

Philip Massinger

376. All excellent things are as difficult as they are rare.

Anon.

377. I do the very best I know how, the very best I can do; and I mean to keep on doing it to the end. If the end brings me out all right, what is said against me won't amount to anything. If the end brings me out all wrong, then angels swearing I was right would make no difference.

Abraham Lincoln

378. Security is mostly a superstition. It does not exist in nature. Life is either a daring adventure or nothing.

Helen Keller

379. We are made to persist. That's how we find out who we are.

Tobias Wolff

380. Rule No. 1: Never lose money. Rule No. 2: Never forget Rule No. 1.

Warren Buffett

381. Accept challenges so you may feel the exhilaration of success.

Anon.

Wise Words

382. Great successes are built on taking the negatives in your life and turning them around.
Sumner Redstone

383. If you do not ask, the answer is always no.
Owen Laughlin

384. He who fears being conquered is sure of defeat.
Napoleon Bonaparte

385. Responsibility educates.
Wendell Phillips

386. Don't undertake a project unless it is manifestly important and nearly impossible.
Edwin H. Land

387. There is no magic in small ideas.
Anon.

388. An expert is someone called in at the last minute to share the blame.
Sam Ewing

389. If you want to truly understand something, try to change it.
Kurt Lewin

390. A long dispute means that both parties are wrong.
Voltaire

Wise Words

391. The past should be a springboard, not a hammock.

Ivern Ball

392. Half the failures in life arise from pulling in one's horse as he is leaping.

Anon.

393. I always wanted to be somebody, but I see now I should have been more specific.

Lily Tomlin

394. Being rich is having money; being wealthy is having time.

Stephen Swid

395. A leader is trusted. A leader takes the initiative. A leader uses good judgment. A leader speaks with authority. A leader strengthens others. A leader is optimistic and enthusiastic. A leader never compromises his absolutes. A leader leads by example.

Mike Abrashoff

396. Accomplishing the impossible means only that the boss will add it to your regular duties.

Doug Larson

397. It is often hard to distinguish between the hard knocks in life and those of opportunity.

Frederick Phillips

Wise Words

398. Money doesn't change men, it merely unmasks them. If a man is naturally selfish or arrogant or greedy, the money brings that out, that is all.
Henry Ford

399. More people would learn from their mistakes if they weren't so busy denying they made them.
Anon.

400. Work is hard if you're paid to do it, and it's a pleasure if you pay to be allowed to do it.
Finley P. Dunne

401. Rest is a good thing, but boredom is its brother.
Voltaire

402. Nothing gives one person so much advantage over another as to remain always cool and unruffled under all circumstances.
Thomas Jefferson

403. Winning has a joy and discrete purity to it that cannot be replaced by anything else.
A. Bartlett Giamatti

404. When you do something you've never done, no matter how poorly it turns out, you're on your way to doing it better the next time.
Anon.

405. Research is to see what everybody else has seen, and to think what nobody else has thought.
Albert Szent-Gyorgyi

Wise Words

406. The secret to happiness: figure out who you are, where you want to go and how you're going to get there...and enjoy the moment.

Marty Edelston

407. Be bold. The cautious will be chewed up!

Bill Bradley

408. I've always observed that to succeed in the world, one should seem a fool but be wise.

Montesquieu

409. Where large sums of money are concerned, it is advisable to trust nobody.

Agatha Christie

410. If it works, copy it.

Tony Schwartz

411. The trouble with the world is that the stupid are cocksure and the intelligent are full of doubt.

Bertrand Russell

412. Yesterday's gone down the river, and you can't get it back.

Larry McMurty

413. Optimism is the content of small men in high places.

F. Scott Fitzgerald

Wise Words

414.   The reasonable man adapts himself to the world; the unreasonable one persists in trying to adapt the world to himself. Therefore, all progress depends upon the unreasonable man.

George Bernard Shaw

415.   Boldness becomes rarer, the higher the rank.

Karl von Clausewitz

416.   The man who views the world at 50 the way as he did at 20 has wasted 30 years of life.

Muhammad Ali

417.   Ideas are funny things. They never work unless you do.

Anon.

418.   A person who has not done one-half his day's work by ten o-clock, runs a chance of leaving the other half undone.

Emily Bronte

419.   Where there is no vision, the people perish.

Proverbs 29:18

420.   Many a man's profanity has saved him from a nervous breakdown.

Henry. S. Haskins

Wise Words

421. Fortunate, indeed, is the man who takes exactly the right measure of himself and holds a just balance between what he can acquire and what he can use.
                           Peter Latham

422. People ask how can a Jewish kid from the Bronx do preppy clothes? Does it have to do with class and money? It has to do with dreams.
                           Ralph Lauren

423. The rule of life that all should know: first comes income, then goes outgo.
                           Cecil Baxter

424. It can't be done, so I did it.
                           Spring Sirkin

425. They call you stubborn when you fail, but persistent when you succeed.
                           Anon.

426. The first rule of holes: when you're in one, stop digging.
                           Molly Ivins

427. Like lemmings jumping off a cliff, the mindless pursuit of even good ideas can be destructive.
                           John R. Hayes

428. It ain't braggin' if you can do it.
                           Dizzy Dean

Wise Words

429. If you don't know all the things you can't do, you can do them.

John Peterman

430. The difference between genius and stupidity is that genius has its limits.

Anon.

431. The lack of something to feel important about is almost the greatest tragedy a man may have.

Arthur E. Morgan

432. You don't make decisions because they are easy; you don't make them because they are cheap; you don't make them because they're popular; you make them because they're right.

Theodore Hesburgh

433. Glory is fleeting, but obscurity is forever.

Napoleon Bonaparte

434. It's time to realize the power you have.

Anon.

435. Anger is a wind which blows out the lamp of the mind.

Robert G. Ingersoll

436. Anyone can make a mistake. A fool insists on repeating it.

Robertine Maynard

Wise Words

437. If people never did silly things, nothing smart would be done.

Ludwig Wittgenstein

438. Education is the progressive discovery of our ignorance.

Will Durant

439. One half of knowing what you want is knowing what you must give up before you get it.

Sidney Howard

440. Courage is resistance to fear, mastery of fear -- not absence of fear.

Mark Twain

441. Creative minds have always been known to survive any kind of bad training.

Anna Freud

442. He's no failure. He's not dead yet.

William Lloyd George

443. The art of being wise is the art of knowing what to overlook.

William James

444. Be the change you want to see in the world.

Mohandas K. Gandhi

445. What happens when the future has come and gone?

Robert Half

Wise Words

446. Whatever you do, you need courage. Whatever course you decide upon, there is always someone to tell you that you are wrong. There are always difficulties arising that tempt you to believe your critics are right. To map out a course of action and follow it to the end requires some of the same courage that soldiers need.

Ralph Waldo Emerson

447. If you hear a voice within you saying, "You are not a painter," then by all means paint, and that voice will be silenced.

Vincent Van Gogh

448. People wish to learn to swim, and at the same time to keep one foot on the ground.

Marcel Proust

449. If you would win a man to your cause, first convince him that you are his sincere friend.

Abraham Lincoln

450. It's better to be a lion for a day than a sheep all your life.

Elizabeth Kenny

451. Politeness and consideration for others is like investing pennies and getting dollars back.

Thomas Sowell

452. A mind, like a home, is furnished by its owner, so if one's life is cold and bare, he can blame none but himself.

Louis L'Amour

Wise Words

453. It's easy to get good players. Getting 'em to play together, that's the hard part.
Casey Stengel

454. Remember that credit is money.
Benjamin Franklin

455. The world stands aside to let anyone pass who knows where he is going.
David S. Jordan

456. Don't make friends who are comfortable to be with. Make friends who will force you to lever yourself up.
Thomas J. Watson, Sr.

457. Silence is the ultimate weapon of power.
Charles De Gaulle

458. Just when you think you've graduated from the school of experience, someone thinks up a new course.
Mary H. Waldrip

459. Little minds are tamed and subdued by misfortunes; great minds rise above them.
Washington Irving

460. In every affair consider what precedes and what follows. Then undertake it.
Epictitus

Wise Words

461.   If you risk nothing, then you risk everything.
Geena Davis

462.   It's what you learn after you know it all that counts.
Anon.

463.   When we seek the best in others, we bring out our best.
William A. Ward

464.   Enjoy the little things in life, for one day you may look back and realize they were the big things.
Robert Brault

465.   A good plan executed right now is far better than a perfect plan executed next week.
George S. Patton, Jr.

466.   Sometimes roads less traveled are less traveled for a reason.
Jerry Seinfeld

467.   My interest is in the future because I'm going to spend the rest of my life there.
Charles Kettering

468.   A genius is a talented person who does his homework.
Thomas A. Edison

469.   Anger consumes; thinking controls.
Anon.

Wise Words

470. The most important thing in communication is to hear what isn't being said.
Peter F. Drucker

471. There's no secret about success. Did you ever know a successful man who didn't tell you about it?
Frank McKinney "Kin" Hubbard

472. When I stand before God at the end of my life, I would hope that I would not have a single bit of talent left but could say, "I used everything you gave me."
Erma Brombeck

473. Never ruin an apology with an excuse.
Kimberly Johnson

474. If you really want to do something, you'll find a way; if you don't, you'll find an excuse.
Anon.

475. What really matters is what you do with what you have.
Shirley Lord

476. I not only use all the brains I have, but all I can borrow.
Woodrow Wilson

477. Change starts when someone sees the next step.
William Drayton

Wise Words

478. Life is like riding a bicycle. You don't fall off unless you stop pedaling.
Claude Pepper

479. Wanting to work is so rare a want that it should be encouraged.
Abraham Lincoln

480. To be a champ, you have to believe in yourself when nobody else will.
Sugar Ray Robinson

481. If the idea is good, it will survive defeat. It may even survive victory.
Stephen Vincent Benet

482. When you have spoken the word, it reigns over you. When it is unspoken, you reign over it.
Arabian proverb

483. The two things people want more than sex or money are recognition and praise.
Mary Kay Ash

484. Men of genius do not excel in a profession because they labor in it; they labor in it because they excel.
William Hazlitt

485. Whether you think you can or think you can't, you're right.
Anon.

Wise Words

486. A good idea is a terrible thing to waste. If you happen to succeed, make sure you've got the resources to succeed on a large scale.
Bob Ackerman

487. Experience is the comb that Nature gives us after we are bald.
Belgian proverb

488. No man lives without jostling and being jostled. In all things he has to elbow himself through the world, giving and receiving offense.
Plautus

489. I like thinking big. If you're going to be thinking anything, you might as well think big.
Donald Trump

490. He not busy being born is busy dying.
Bob Dylan

491. Lead with ideas and people will follow.
Anon.

492. Whatever you do, or dream you can do, begin it. Boldness has genius, power and magic in it.
Goethe

493. The man who damns money has obtained it dishonorably; the man who respect is has earned it.
Ayn Rand

Wise Words

494. I've never been poor, only broke. Being poor is a frame of mind. Being broke is only a temporary situation.
Mike Todd

495. If you don't risk anything, you risk even more.
Erica Jong

496. Success is never sufficient.
Robert Half

497. Most plans are just inaccurate predictions.
Ben Bayol

498. This is as true in everyday life as it is in battle: we are given one life and the decision is ours whether to wait for circumstances to make up our mind or whether to act and, in acting, to live.
Omar M. Bradley

499. Today's mighty oak is just yesterday's nut that held its ground.
Anon.

500. If at first you don't succeed, you are running about average.
M.H. Alderson

501. Without ambition one starts nothing. Without work one finishes nothing.
Ralph Waldo Emerson

Wise Words

502. When you go in search of honey, you must expect to be stung by bees.
Kenneth Kaunda

503. When you want to fool the world, tell the truth.
Otto Von Bismark

504. Remember, amateurs built the ark. Professionals build the Titanic.
Anon.

505. I have learned to use the word "impossible" with the greatest caution.
Wernher von Braun

506. If a man doesn't keep pace with his companions, perhaps it is because he hears a different drummer.
Henry David Thoreau

507. Only a fool tests the depth of the water with both feet.
African Proverb

508. A new idea is delicate. It can be killed by a sneer or a yawn; it can be stabbed to death by a joke, or worried to death by a frown on the right person's brow.
Charles Brower

509. Success is not permanent. The same is also true of failure.
Anon.

Wise Words

510. I always believe in me. The guy who succeeds is the guy who says, "I'm going to succeed."
John Peterman

511. When you reach for the stars, you may not quite get one, but you won't come up with a handful of mud either.
Leo Burnett

512. If you act in usual ways, you won't get anywhere.
Henri Termeer

513. Sometimes you just have to take a chance – and correct your mistakes as you go along.
Lee Iacocca

514. The best way I know to win an argument is to start by being right.
Lord Hailsham

515. Creativity demands more than a good idea.
John C. Jay

516. Prudence is the necessary ingredient in all the virtues, that without which they degenerate into folly and excess.
Jeremy Collier

517. Nothing is more difficult, and therefore more precious, than to be able to decide.
Napoleon Bonaparte

Wise Words

518. The essential factor that lifts one man above his fellows in terms of achievement and success is his capacity for greater self-discipline.
Ray Kroc

519. To acquire knowledge, one must study; but to acquire wisdom, one must observe.
Marilyn von Savant

520. All husbands are alike, but they have different faces so you can tell them apart.
Anon.

521. Laughter gives us distance. It allows us to step back from an event, deal with it, then move on.
Bob Newhart

522. All animals except man know that the principal business of life is to enjoy it.
Samuel Butler

523. There is more to life than increasing its speed.
Mohandas K. Gandhi

524. What we anticipate seldom occurs; what we least expect generally happens.
Benjamin Disraeli

525. We haven't the money, so we've got to think.
Lord Rutherford

Wise Words

526. When you are making a success of something, it's not work. It's a way of life.
Andy Granatelli

527. If you're going to soar like an eagle, you have to work like a dog.
Anon.

528. You can only lead by example. A real leader doesn't blow his own horn. He's judged by the actions he takes, and by results.
Don Mattingly

529. The world is your playground. Why aren't you playing?
Ellie Katz

530. When a thing is not worth overdoing, leave it alone.
Henry S. Haskings

531. By the time we recognize an opportunity, it has ceased to be one.
Mark Twain

532. Ye shall know the truth, and the truth shall make you mad.
Aldous Huxley

533. One must learn the lessons of the past. But the path of success requires that these lessons be treated only as stepping stones to the future.
Edward Nash

Wise Words

534. A wish is a desire without an attempt.

Anon.

535. One person with a belief is equal to a force of ninety-nine who have only interests.

John Stewart Mill

536. The way to love anything is to realize that it might be lost.

G.K. Chesterton

537. It is better to be defeated on principle than to win on lies.

Arthur Calwell

538. Failing to prepare is preparing to fail.

John Wooden

539. It's OK to work on an idea that doesn't work out, as long as we've made it as good as we can make it.

Marty Edelston

540. There is only one thing more painful than learning from experience, and that's not learning from experience.

Archibald MacLeish

541. Before everything else, getting ready is the secret of success.

Henry Ford

Wise Words

542.   It give me great pleasure, indeed, to see the stubbornness of an incorrigible nonconformist warmly acclaimed.
Albert Einstein

543.   I wish I could stand on a busy street corner, hat in hand, and beg people to throw me all their wasted hours.
Bernard Berenson

544.   Wisdom is the reward you get from a lifetime of listening when you'd have preferred to talk.
Doug Larson

545.   A man who dares to waste an hour of his life has not discovered the value of life.
Charles Darwin

546.   Life's longest mile is from dependence to independence.
Carla B. James

547.   In the realm of ideas, everything depends on enthusiasm; in the real world, all rests on perseverance.
Goethe

548.   What are you gonna do? Something! Who are you gonna be? Somebody!
Philip Frostburg

549.   This is the difference between being smart and being wise: smart people learn from their experience; wise people learn from the experience of others.
Ichak Adizes

Wise Words

550. Moderation is a fatal thing; nothing succeeds like excess.

Oscar Wilde

551. A man's worst difficulties begin when he is able to do what he likes.

Thomas Huxley

552. I can't change the direction of the wind, but I can adjust my sails to always reach my destination.

Jimmy Dean

553. The chains of habit are generally too small to be felt until they are too strong to be broken.

Samuel Johnson

554. Aim for perfection! Half right is always half wrong.

Anon.

555. Imagination is the true magic carpet.

Norman Vincent Peale

556. Persistent people know they can succeed where smarter and more talented people fail.

Suzanne Chazin

557. The pessimist complains about the wind; the optimist expects it to change; the realist adjusts the sails.

William A. Ward

Wise Words

558.   When you're at the end of your rope, tie a knot and hang on.

Theodore Roosevelt

559.   Our greatest weakness lies in giving up. The most certain way to succeed is to always try just one more time.

Thomas A. Edison

560.   Always assume that the risk you don't see is much greater than the risk you do see.

Anon.

561.   The man who has no imagination has no wings.

Muhammad Ali

562.   Nothing gets done unless you start somewhere.

Carolyn T. Geer

563.   There is no substitute for a passionate dreamer with a good idea and the drive to see it realized.

Leslie Bennette

564.   Fortune befriends the bold.

John Dryden

565.   There is always some risk when you try something you've never done. But that risk is outweighed.by the challenge of creating a well-planned effort, by the strength and experience gained from trying, and by the feelings of satisfaction and pride that come with success.

Philip A. Grisolia

Wise Words

566. The Lord gave each of us two ends to use; one to think with, one to sit on. What we become depends on which end we choose. Heads we win, tails we lose.

Anon.

567. The prize will not be sent to you. You have to win it.

Ralph Waldo Emerson

568. Experience is knowing a lot of things you shouldn't do.

William S. Knudsen

569. The young don't recognized the impossible because they've never met it.

Ray Sons

570. The difference between a successful person and others is not a lack of strength, not a lack of knowledge, but rather a lack of will.

Vince Lombardi

571. I not only use all the brains I have, but all I can borrow.

Woodrow Wilson

572. Conform and be dull.

J. Frank Doble

573. By perseverance the snail reached the ark.

Charles Spurgeon

Wise Words

574. No pressure, no diamonds.

Mary Case

575. You may be disappointed if you fail, but you are doomed if you don't try.

Beverly Sills

576. To think too long about doing a thing becomes its undoing.

Eva Young

577. Progress in life is not measured by security, but by growth; and growth means taking occasional risks. You'll never get anywhere interesting by always doing the same thing.

Anon.

578. When you cannot make up your mind which of two evenly balanced courses of action you should take – choose the bolder.

W.J. Slim

579. To try and fail is at least to learn. To fail to try is to suffer the inestimable loss of what might have been.

Chester Bernard

580. We either find a way, or make one.

Hannibal

581. Failures provide the lessons to ensure progress.

Nihachiro Katayama

Wise Words

582. Beware of the man who won't be bothered with details.
William Feather

583. Top cats begin as underdogs.
Bernard Meltzer

584. Each man's task is his life preserver.
George B. Emerson

585. What you want to do you do. The rest is just talk.
John Cleek

586. Experience is the worst teacher. It gives the test before presenting the lesson.
Vernon Law

587. To bear up under loss, to fight the bitterness of defeat and the weakness of grief, to be victor over anger, to smile when tears are close, resist evil men and base instincts, to hate hate and to love love, to go on when it would seem good to die, to seek ever after the glory and the dream, to look up with the unquenchable faith in something evermore about to be, that is what any man can do, and so be great.
Zane Grey

588. Vision is the art of seeing things invisible.
Jonathan Swift

589. Throughout history, the most common debilitating human ailment has been cold feet.
Anon.

Wise Words

590. If you pray for rain, don't be surprised if you're stuck by lightning.
Damien Cannon

591. I am a firm believer in luck. The harder I work, the more of it I seem to have.
Coleman Cox

592. Great minds have purpose, others have wishes.
Washington Irving

593. Experiences are savings which a miser puts aside. Wisdom is an inheritance which a wastrel cannot exhaust.
Karl Kraus

594. Success breeds self-confidence.
Nihachiro Katayama

595. Don't wait for your ship to come in. Swim out to it.
Anon.

596. An error is simply a failure to adjust immediately from a preconception to an actuality.
John Cage

597. In business, the competition will bite you if you keep running; if you stand still, they will swallow you.
William S. Knudsen

Wise Words

598. Behold the turtle: He only makes progress when he sticks his neck out.

James B. Conant

599. What people say you cannot do, you try and find that you can.

Henry David Thoreau

600. Ignorance is curable. Stupidity is not.

Anon.

601. Small opportunities are often the beginning of great enterprises.

Demosthenes

602. A belief is not merely an idea the mind possesses; it is an idea that possesses the mind.

Robert Bolton

603. If you want to succeed, you should strike out on new paths rather than travel the worn paths of accepted success.

John D. Rockefeller, Jr.

604. The talent of success is nothing more than doing what you can do well, and doing well whatever you do.

Longfellow

605. The only way to coast is down hill.

Anon.

Wise Words

606. The man who knows how will always have a job. The man who also knows why will always be his boss.

Ralph Waldo Emerson

607. Failure is the opportunity to begin again more intelligently.

Henry Ford

608. Most of us ask for advice when we know the answer but want a different one.

Ivern Ball

609. What we see depends mainly on what we look for.

Anon.

610. Some is better than none; more is better than some.

Glen Taylor

611. Well begun is half done.

English Proverb

612. Establishing goals is alright if you don't let them deprive you of interesting detours.

Doug Larson

613. To err is human, but when the eraser wears out ahead of the pencil, you're overdoing it.

J. Jenkins

Wise Words

614. Entrepreneurs should be realists, not optimists. Optimists always look for the light at the end of the tunnel; realists look for the next tunnel.
Tom Golisano

615. When a man is willing and eager, the gods join in.
Aeschylus

616. Despite the success cult, men are most deeply moved not by the reaching of the goal but by the grandness of effort involved in getting there – or failing to get there.
Max Lerner

617. The secret of making money in business: Know something nobody else knows.
Aristotle Onassis

618. The race is not always to the swift; it is to those who keep running.
Anon.

619. The power of imagination makes us infinite.
John Muir

620. The man who ain't got an enemy is really poor.
Josh Billings

621. Wise men learn more from fools than fools from the wise.
Cato

Wise Words

622. The right time to get into any field is when the market's perception is that the time is wrong.

Paul Reichmann

623. Never be afraid to admit you were wrong. It's like saying you're wiser today than you were yesterday.

Anon.

624. The dictionary is the only place where success comes before work.

Arthur Brisbane

625. The biggest enemy is doubt. If you don't believe in what you are doing, you aren't going to make it.

Philippe Kahn

626. The wise man will make more opportunities than he finds.

Francis Bacon

627. It is not enough to have a good mind. The main thing is to use it well.

Rene Descartes

628. Some mistakes are too much fun to make only once.

Anon.

629. There is always danger for those who are afraid of it.

George Bernard Shaw

Wise Words

630. Without risk, nothing good happens.

Alex Kroll

631. Education will never become as expensive as ignorance.

Anon.

632. Difficulties are things that show what men are.

Epictitus

633. No victor believes in chance.

Friedrich Nietzsche

634. The four cornerstones of character on which this nation is built are: Initiative, Imagination, Individuality and Independence.

Edward Rickenbacker

635. Those who pay peanuts will employ only monkeys.

Philip Frostburg

636. The best way to reduce risk is to address its causes rather than its effects.

Theodore W. Barnes

637. The fellow who never makes a mistake takes his orders from one who does.

Herbert V. Prochnow

638. The mass of men lead lives of quiet desperation.

Henry David Thoreau

Wise Words

639. Always view problems as opportunities in work clothes.

Henry J. Kaiser

640. Not taking risks may be the biggest risk of all.

Anon.

641. Personal character, like any seed, needs a decent environment in which to develop.

Parker W. Silzer

642. A good idea wrapped in a lot of loose ends is in reality a bad idea.

Anon.

643. Common senses is instinct. Enough of it is genius.

Josh Billings

644. Laziness is a secret ingredient that goes into failure. But it's only kept a secret from the person who fails.

Robert Half

645. Freedom is nothing else but a chance to be better.

Albert Camus

646. Kites rise highest against the wind, not with it.

Winston Churchill

Wise Words

647. Against the impact of new ideas, there is no defense except stupidity.
>> Anon.

648. To be an entrepreneur is to not be afraid to fail.
>> Philip N. Knight

649. Well-married, a man is winged; ill-matched, he is shackled.
>> Henry Ward Beecher

650. The very substance of the ambitious is merely the shadow of a dream.
>> William Shakespeare

651. Achievers may lose their jobs, get rejected, watch their companies fail, or see their ideas founder. But they take advantage of adversity, carving opportunities from change.
>> Suzanne Chazin

652. The poor man is not he who is without a cent, but he who is without a dream.
>> Anon.

653. Hindsight is an exact science.
>> Guy Bellamy

654. Some things get done badly because they are genuinely hard to do well, and some get done badly because nobody tried hard enough to do them well.
>> Eileen Shanahan

Wise Words

655. The hardest things to handle in life are failure and success.
Anon.

656. Ignorance is voluntary misfortune.
Nicholas Ling

657. Knowledge is like money. The more you get, the more you crave.
Josh Billings

658. The real value of any new idea is in direct proportion to the size of the problem it will solve.
Anon.

659. They conquer who believe they can.
John Dryden

660. Goals are dreams with deadlines.
Diana S. Hunt

661. The principle mark of genius is not perfection but originality, the opening of new frontiers.
Arthur Koestler

662. Self-respect permeates every aspect of your life.
Joe Clark

663. Adversity introduces a man to himself.
Anon.

Wise Words

664. To sit back and let fate play its hand out and never influence it is not the way man was meant to operate.
John Glenn

665. With ignorance and confidence, success is sure.
Mark Twain

666. Few wishes come true by themselves.
June Smith

667. One thing about experience is that when you don't have very much you're apt to get a lot.
Franklin P. Jones

668. Between the great things that we cannot do and the small things we will not do, the danger is that we shall do nothing.
Adolph Monod

669. Some people never hear opportunity knock because they're too busy knocking opportunity.
Hal Chadwick

670. Don't cry because it's over; smile because it happened.
Anon.

671. It takes as much courage to have tried and failed as it does to have tried and succeeded.
Anne Morrow Lindbergh

672. Opportunity's favorite disguise is trouble.
Frank Tyger

Wise Words

673.   **S**ome things have to be believed to be seen.

Ralph Hodgson

674.   **A**im high! It is no harder to shoot the feathers off an eagle than it is to shoot the fur off a skunk.

Troy Moore

675.   **D**on't let what you cannot do interfere with what you can.

John Wooden

676.   **D**iscipline is remembering what you want.

David Campbell

677.   **P**essimism never won any battle.

Dwight D. Eisenhower

678.   **S**tart by doing what's necessary, then what's possible, and suddenly you are doing the impossible.

St. Francis of Assisi

679.   **T**he optimist thinks that this is the best possible world. The pessimist fears that this is true.

Anon.

680.   **W**ho gives up when behind is cowardly. Who gives up when ahead is foolish.

William A. Ward

Wise Words

681. There is a time to let things happen and a time to make things happen.
Hugh Prather

682. There is a lot to be said for the fellow who doesn't say it himself.
Maurice Switzer

683. Ambition is the germ from which all growth of nobleness proceeds.
Thomas D. English

684. The only way to discover the limits of the possible is to go beyond them into the impossible.
Arthur C. Clarke

685. It's not what you know, it's what you do with what you know that counts.
Anon.

686. There is only one success – to spend your life in your own way.
Christopher Morley

687. Nature creates ability; luck provides it with opportunity.
Francois de La Rochefouchauld

688. There is no more miserable human being than one in whom nothing is habitual but indecision.
Euripides

Wise Words

689. Just because no one else has done it yet does not mean you can't.
Philip A. Grisolia

690. Action, to be effective, must be directed to clearly conceived ends.
Jawaharial Nehru

691. If at first you don't succeed, try again. Then quit! There's no use being a damned fool about it.
W.C. Fields

692. Success is getting what you want; happiness is wanting what you get.
Anon.

693. If you always know exactly what you want, that will be the most you will ever find.
Pablo Picasso

694. A problem well stated is a problem half solved.
Charles Kettering

695. The fact that an opinion has been widely held is no evidence whatever that it is not entirely absurd.
Bertrand Russell

696. An invasion of armies can be resisted, but not an idea whose time has come.
Victor Hugo

Wise Words

697. Few enterprises of great labor or hazard would be undertaken if we had not the power of magnifying the advantages we expect from them.
Samuel Johnson

698. Make money your God and it will plague you like the devil.
Henry Fielding

699. Destiny is no matter of chance. It is a matter of choice. It is not a thing to be waited for. It is a thing to be achieved.
William Jennings Bryan

700. Anyone who stops learning is old, whether at twenty or eighty. Anyone who keeps learning stays young. The greatest thing in life is to keep your mind young.
Henry Ford

701. Your success depends upon you. You have to steer your own course, build your own monument – or dig your own pit.
B.C. Forbes

702. He will always be a slave who does not know how to live upon a little.
Horace

703. Imagination is more important than knowledge.
Albert Einstein

Wise Words

704. The differences between men's abilities are not nearly so great as the differences between their accomplishments.

Anon.

705. Luck is what happens when preparation meets opportunity.

Elmer Letterman

706. If one advances confidently in the direction of his dreams, and endeavors to lead the life which he has imagined, he will meet with success.

Henry David Thoreau

707. Never tell anyone how to do things. Tell them what to do and they will surprise you with their ingenuity.

George S. Patton, Jr.

708. You can't cross the sea merely by standing and staring at the water. Don't let yourself indulge in vain wishes.

Rabindranath Tagore

709. If you have made mistakes, even serious ones, there is always another chance for you. What we call failure is not the falling down, but the staying down.

Mary Pickford

Wise Words

710. When you are aspiring to the highest place, it is honorable to reach the second or even the third rank.

Cicero

711. We can learn a lot from crayons. Some are sharp, others dull. Some are pretty, others have strange names. And while all are different colors, they exist nicely in the same box.

Anon.

712. Think wrongly, if you please, but in all cases think for yourself.

Doris Lessing

713. I don't think winning is the most important thing. I think winning is the only thing.

Bill Veeck

714. The nice thing about teamwork is that you always have others on your side.

Margaret Carty

715. All men of action are dreamers.

James G. Huneker

716. High aims form high character, and great objectives bring out great minds.

Byron Edwards

717. Restlessness and discontent are the necessities of progress.

Thomas A. Edison

Wise Words

718. Age doesn't always bring wisdom. Sometimes age comes alone.
Anon.

719. He is rich or poor according to what he is, not according to what he has.
Henry Ward Beecher

720. The more we do, the more we can do.
William Hazlitt

721. At least half the exercise I get every day comes from jumping to conclusions.
Bruce B. Dexter

722. Every crowd has a silver lining.
P.T. Barnum

723. Just about the time you make both ends meet, somebody moves the ends.
Pansy Penner

724. The dissenter is every human being at those moments of his life when he retires momentarily from the herd and thinks for himself.
Archibald MacLeish

725. Risk surrounds everything worth accomplishing.
Anon.

Wise Words

726. The trouble in American life today, in business as well as in sports, is that too many people are afraid of competition.
Knute Rockne

727. Indecision is debilitating. It feeds upon itself. It is, one might almost say, habit-forming. Not only that, but it is contagious. It transmits itself to others.
H.A. Hopf

728. We may lay in a stock of pleasures, as we would lay in a stock of wine, but if we defer tasting them too long we shall find that both are soured by age.
Charles C. Colton

729. The final test of a leader is that he leaves behind him in other men the conviction and the will to carry on.
Walter Lippmann

730. It is difficult to say what is impossible, for the dream of yesterday is the hope of today and the reality of tomorrow.
Robert H. Goddard

731. You don't drown by falling in the water; you drown by staying there.
Edwin Louis Cole

732. A man who has committed a mistake and doesn't correct it is committing another mistake.
Confucius

Wise Words

733. If you wish to make enemies, tell people simply, "You are wrong." This method works every time.
Henry C. Link

734. Insist on yourself; never imitate.
Ralph Waldo Emerson

735. It is not so important to be serious as it is to be serious about important things.
Robert M. Hutchins

736. Take time to deliberate, but when the time for actions arrives, stop thinking and go in. One man with courage makes a majority.
Andrew Jackson

737. The first step in solving a problem is to tell someone about it.
John Peter Flynn

738. In the battle for existence, talent is the punch, tact the fancy footwork.
Wilson Mizner

739. There are two kinds of people in the world: those who do the work and those who take credit for it. Try to be in the first group. There is less competition there.
Indira Gandhi

740. You can't plow a field by turning it over in your mind.
Anon.

Wise Words

741. You can buy a man's time, his physical presence at a given place even a measured number of his skilled motions per hour. But you cannot buy enthusiasm, his loyalty or the devotion of his heart, mind or soul. You must earn these.
Clarence Francis.

742. To be conscious that you are ignorant of the facts is a great step toward knowledge.
Benjamin Disraeli

743. It is no use saying, "We are doing our best." You have got to succeed in doing what is necessary.
Winston Churchill

744. The secret of joy in work is contained in one word -- excellence. To know how to do something well is to enjoy it.
Pearl S. Buck

745. Leadership is the ability to get others to do what they don't want to do and like it.
Harry S. Truman

746. Smart is when you believe only half of what you hear. Brilliant is when you know which half to believe.
Orben's Current Comedy

747. Problems create opportunities.
Anon.

Wise Words

748. I'm just a plow hand from Arkansas, but I have learned how to hold a team together, how to lift some men up, how to calm down others, until finally they've got one heartbeat together, a team. There's just three things I'd ever say: If anything goes bad, I did it. If anything goes semi-good, then we did it. If anything goes real good, then you did it. That's all it takes to get people to win for you.
Bear Bryant

749. Begin where you are, but above all begin. Act. Move forward. There can be no progress when you march in place.
Philip Frostburg

750. Experience is the name everyone gives to his mistakes.
Woodrow Wilson

751. A great teacher never strives to explain his vision. He simply invites you to stand beside him and see for yourself.
R. Inman

752. We all find time to do what we really want to do.
William Feather

753. He that is good for making excuses is seldom good for anything else.
Benjamin Franklin

754. The best thinking has been done in solitude. The worst has been done in turmoil.
Thomas A. Edison

Wise Words

755. Faith is believing in things when common sense tells you not to.
George Seaton

756. The fewer the facts, the stronger the opinion.
Arnold H. Glasgow

757. When your work speaks for itself, don't interrupt.
Anon.

758. The first essential of doing a job well is to wish to see the job done at all.
Franklin D. Roosevelt

759. We must, all of us, dare to be different.
Edward Nash

760. The wise know the value of riches, but the rich do not know the pleasures of wisdom.
Hebrew proverb

761. Be fair with others, but then keep after them until they are fair with you.
Alan Alda

762. The easiest thing to decide is what you would do if you were in someone else's shoes.
Anon.

Wise Words

763. If you think what exists today is permanent and forever true, you inevitably get your head handed to you.

John Reed

764. Wealth is the product of man's capacity to think.

Ayn Rand

765. It's much better to move fast and make mistakes occasionally than to move too slowly.

Juergen Schrempp

766. Money does not make you happy, but it quiets the nerves.

Sean O'Casey

767. The best use of life is to spend it for something that outlasts life.

William James

768. Sometimes you just have to take a chance -- and correct your mistakes as you go along.

Lee Iacocca

769. Wise men learn from other men's mistakes; fools from their own.

Anon.

770. Conscience is what hurts when everything else feels so good.

Anon.

Wise Words

771. Work expands so as to fill the time available for its completion.
        C. Northcote Parkinson

772. When you can do the common things of life in an uncommon way, you will command the attention of the world.
        George Washington Carver

773. Corporations spend a lot of money encouraging people to be creative, while tacitly ensuring just the opposite.
        Arno Penzias

774. Hide from risk and you hide from its reward.
        Anon.

775. There is more to life than increasing its speed.
        Mahatma Gandhi

776. Tact is to lie about others as you would have them lie about you.
        Oliver Herford

777. No competition, no progress.
        Bela Karolyi

778. A teacher affects eternity; he can never tell where his influence stops.
        Henry Brooks Adams

Wise Words

779. There is no genius in life like the genius of activity.
Donald G. Mitchell

780. There is a kind of victory in good work, no matter how humble.
Jack Kemp

781. Don't just spend time. Invest it!
Philip Frostburg

782. A wife is a gift bestowed upon man to reconcile him to the loss of paradise.
Goethe

783. The secret of success is to start from scratch and keep on scratching.
Anon.

784. Insanity is hereditary; you can get if from your children.
Sam Levinson

785. Life consists not in holding good cards, but in playing well those you do hold.
Josh Billings

786. The luck of having talent is not enough; one must also have a talent for luck.
Hector Berloiz

787. Pay your people the least possible and you will get from them the same.
Malcomb S. Forbes

Wise Words

788. Convictions are more dangerous foes of truth than lies.

Friedrich Nietzsche

789. You can't be afraid of stepping on toes if you want to go dancing.

Lewis Freedman

790. Wealth consists not in having great possessions, but in having few wants.

Anon.

791. There is nothing so fatal to character as half-finished tasks.

David Lloyd George

792. Little strokes fell great oaks.

Benjamin Franklin

793. It is often easier to get forgiveness than permission.

Anon.

794. Always remember that if you work at a wrong plan, you are neglecting the right plan, the plan that would accomplish results.

Ed Howe

795. He who makes money pleases God.

Muhammad

Wise Words

796. Tell me what ticks you off, and I will tell you what makes you tick.

Lloyd John Ogilvie

797. Happiness often comes through doors you didn't even know you left open.

Anon.

798. Praise can give criticism a lead around the first turn and still win the race.

Ben Williams

799. The proper function of man is to live – not to exist.

Jack London

800. Successful people understand that no one makes it to the top in a single bound. What truly sets them apart is their willingness to keep putting one step in front of the other -- no matter how rough the terrain.

Suzanne Chazin

801. Performance speaks louder than words.

Anon.

802. The only difference between a rut and a grave is the dimensions.

Ellen Glasgow

803. A man cannot be comfortable without his own approval.

Mark Twain

Wise Words

804. Half the worry in the world is caused by people trying to make decisions before they have sufficient knowledge on which to base them.

Dean Hawkes

805. There is only one way to get anybody to do anything, that is by making the other person want to do it.

Dale Carnegie

806. Common sense is very uncommon.

Horace Greeley

807. Never attribute to malice what can be adequately explained by stupidity.

Anon.

808. What a man thinks of himself, that it is what determines, or rather indicates, his fate.

Henry David Thoreau

809. Our greatest glory consists not in never failing, but in rising every time we fail.

Oliver Goldsmith

810. What the fool does in the end, the wise man does in the beginning.

Proverb

811. There are two ways of meeting difficulties; you alter the difficulties, or you alter yourself meeting them.

Phyllis Bottome

Wise Words

812. One who is content with what he has done will never become famous for what he will do. He has lain down to die, and the grass is already over him.
Christian N. Bovee

813. Hope for the best, but prepare for the worst.
English proverb

814. A leader is a man who assumes responsibility. He says, "I was beaten." He does not say, "My men were beaten."
Antoine de Saint-Exupery

815. The family you come from isn't as important as the family you're going to have.
Ring Lardner

816. All final decisions are made in a state of mind that is not going to last.
Marcel Proust

817. Living well is the best revenge.
Anon.

818. He who never learned to obey cannot be a good commander.
Aristotle

819. Have confidence that if you have done a little thing well, you can do a bigger thing well, too.
Storey

Wise Words

820. Facts do not cease to exist because they are ignored.

Anon.

821. Courage is almost a contradiction in terms. It means a strong desire to live taking the form of readiness to die.

G.K. Chesterton

822. One of the greatest characteristics of genius is that power of lighting its own fire.

John W. Foste

823. A thing worth having is a thing worth cheating for.

W.C. Fields

824. Never mistake motion for action.

Ernest Hemingway

825. He who controls the past commands the future. He who commands the future conquers the past.

George Orwell

826. Success is the sum of small efforts repeated day in and day out.

Robert Collier

827. Become addicted to constant and never ending self-improvement.

Anthony J. D'Angelo

Wise Words

828. To gain that which is worth having, it may be necessary to lose everything else.
Bernadette Devlin

829. It's kind of fun to do the impossible.
Walt Disney

830. There is nothing so useless as doing efficiently that which should not be done at all.
Peter F. Drucker

831. When I discover who I am, I'll be free.
Ralph Ellison

832. Learning is not compulsory. Neither is survival.
W. Edwards Deming

833. Thinking is the hardest work there is, which is probably the reason why so few engage in it.
Henry Ford

834. The world is all gates, all opportunities, strings of tension waiting to be struck.
Ralph Waldo Emerson

835. Even a mosquito doesn't get a slap on the back until he starts working.
Anon.

836. Nothing is more expensive than a start.
Friedrich Nietzsche

Wise Words

837. I never learn anything talking. I only learn things when I ask questions.
Lou Holtz

838. Whoever wants to reach a distant goal must take many small steps.
Helmut Schmidt

839. If you don't want to work, you have to work to earn enough money so that you won't have to work.
Ogden Nash

840. The ablest man I ever met is the man you think you are.
Franklin D. Roosevelt

841. There is no deodorant like success.
Elizabeth Taylor

842. Adversity reveals genius, prosperity conceals it.
Horace

843. Unless each day can be looked back upon by an individual as one in which he has some joy, some real satisfaction, that day is a loss.
Dwight D. Eisenhower

844. The frog at the bottom of a well knows not that great oceans exist.
Chinese proverb

Wise Words

845. Success has nothing to do with what you gain in life or accomplish for yourself. It's what you do for others.

Danny Thomas

846. It is easier to do a job right than to explain why you didn't.

Martin Van Buren

847. Reading to the mind is what exercise is to the body.

Joseph Addison

848. We can only change the world by changing men.

Charles Wells

849. Regret for time wasted can become a power for good in the time that remains.

Arthur Brisbane

850. The best place to succeed is where you are with what you have.

Charles M. Schwab

851. Self-trust is the essence of heroism.

Ralph Waldo Emerson

852. Show me a thoroughly satisfied man and I will show you a failure.

Thomas A. Edison

Wise Words

853. One-third of the people in the Unites States promote, while the other two-thirds provide.

Will Rogers

854. The grand essentials of happiness are: something to do, something to live for, and something to hope for.

Alan K. Chalmers

855. God helps them that help themselves.

Proverb

856. The road to hell is paved with good intentions.

Karl Marx

857. People who do things that count never stop to count them

Anon.

858. Nothing great was ever achieved without enthusiasm.

Ralph Waldo Emerson

859. The secret of success is constancy of purpose.

Benjamin Disraeli

860. That which is called firmness in a king is called obstinacy in a donkey.

Lord Erskine

Wise Words

861.   Big shots are only little shots who keep on shooting.

Christopher Morley

862.   Pessimism is only the name that men of weak nerves give to wisdom.

Bernard De Voto

863.   Men never think in crowds. In crowds they are governed by the animal heard instinct, which is directly and powerfully opposed to the thinking principle.

B.C. Forbes

864.   I have great faith in fools -- self-confidence, my friends call it.

Edgar Allan Poe

865.   Poverty is the step-mother of genius.

Josh Billings

866.   Calamity is the perfect glass wherein we truly see and know ourselves.

William Davenant

867.   The dynamo of our economic system is self-interest, which may range from mere petty greed to admirable types of self-expression.

Felix Frankfurter

868.   The first half of life consists of the capacity to enjoy with the chance to do so; the last half consists of the chance without the capacity.

Mark Twain

Wise Words

869. He who has imagination without learning has wings and no feet.
Joseph Joubert

870. There are two tragedies in life. One is to not get your heart's desire, the other is to get it.
George Bernard Shaw

871. To accomplish great things, you must not only act but also dream, not only dream but also believe.
Anatole France

872. Great thoughts reduced to practice become great acts.
William Hazlitt

873. It will generally be found that men who are constantly lamenting their ill luck are only reaping the consequences of their own neglect, mismanagement and improvidence, or want of application.
Samuel Smiles

874. The universe is full of magical things patiently waiting for our wits to grow sharper.
Eden Philpotts

875. In everything the middle course is best; all things in excess bring trouble.
Plautus

876. Experience is a comb that life gives you after you lose your hair.
Judith Stern

Wise Words

877. The reward of a thing well done is to have it done.

Ralph Waldo Emerson

878. It is surprising what a man can do when he has to, and how little most men will do when they don't have to.

William Pitt

879. Things don't turn up in this world until somebody turns them up.

James Garfield

880. Be braver. You can't cross a chasm in two small jumps

David Lloyd George

881. Every man is the architect of his own fortune.

Sallust

882. It is more than probable that the average man could, with no injury to his health, increase his efficiency fifty percent.

Walter Scott

883. Where there is the necessary technical skill to move mountains there is no need for the faith that moves mountains.

Eric Hoffer

884. Lots of people know a good thing the minute the other fellow sees it first.

Joe E. Hedges

Wise Words

885. The end of wisdom is to dream high enough to lose the dream in the seeking of it.

William Faulkner

886. Them that can do; them that can't haven't tried.

Anon.

887. Let no one be ashamed to say "yes" today if yesterday he said "no." Or to say "no" today if yesterday he said "yes," for that is life. Never to have changed – what a pitiable thing of which to boast.

Goethe

888. Disappointment is the nurse of wisdom.

Boyle Roche

889. When you have to make a choice and don't make it, that in itself is a choice.

William James

890. It doesn't matter how new an idea is; it matters how new it becomes.

Elias Canetti

891. Better to wear out than to rust out.

Richard Cumberland

Wise Words

892. The men who succeed are the efficient few. They are the few who have the ambition and will power to develop themselves.

Herbert N. Casson

893. There is no advancement to him who stands trembling because he cannot see the end from the beginning.

E.J. Klemme

894. Mine is better than ours.

Benjamin Franklin

895. Endurance is patience concentrated.

Thomas Carlyle

896. Let him who would move the world first move himself.

Socrates

897. In politics, an absurdity is not a handicap.

Napoleon Bonaparte

898. Thought takes man out of servitude into freedom.

Longfellow

899. People do not lack strength; they lack will.

Victor Hugo

Wise Words

900. Every man who observes vigilantly and resolves steadfastly grows unconsciously into genius.

E.G. Bulwer-Lytton

901. When all else is lost, the future still remains.

Christian N. Bovee

902. If we begin with certainties, we shall end in doubts; but if we begin with doubts, and we are patient in them, we shall end in certainties.

Francis Bacon

903. Gain is gain, however small.

Robert Browning

904. Though you may be only one person in a world full of other people, you can easily be the world to one other person.

Anon.

905. It is never safe to look into the future with eyes of fear.

Edward H. Harriman

906. Better lose the anchor than the whole ship.

Dutch proverb

907. Every noble work is at first impossible.

Thomas Carlyle

Wise Words

908. A happy person is one who enjoys the scenery on a detour.

Anon.

909. There are two kinds of men who never amount to much: those who cannot do what they are told, and those who can do nothing else.

Cyrus H. Curtis

910. Uncertainty and expectation are the joys of life.

William Congreve

911. True courage is like a kite: a contrary wind raises it higher.

J. Petit-Senn

912. The average person puts only 25% of his energy and ability into his work. The world takes of its hat to those who put in more than 50% of their capacity, and stands on its head for those few and far between souls who devote 100%.

Andrew Carnegie

913. Everything comes to him who hustles while he waits.

Thomas A. Edison

914. Do not attempt to do a thing unless you are sure of yourself; but do not give it up simply because someone else is not sure of you.

Steward E. White

915. Fanaticism is the false fire of an overheated mind.

William Cowper

Wise Words

916. **D**ifficulties strengthen the mind as labor does the body.
Seneca

917. **O**ur strength grows out of our weakness.
Ralph Waldo Emerson

918. **L**ogic, like whiskey, loses its beneficial effect when taken in too large a quantity.
Lord Dunsany

919. **A** really good idea is actually just a midwife to an even better one.
Alice Ward Jones

920. **A** theory is no more like a fact than a photograph is like a person.
Ed Howe

921. **O**ld minds are like old horses; you must exercise them if you wish to keep them in working order.
John Quincy Adams

922. **I**t's hard to get toothpaste back in the tube once you let it out.
Anon.

923. **I**magination rules the world.
Napoleon Bonaparte

924. **N**othing is more dangerous than an idea when it is the only one we have.
Alain

Wise Words

925. The surrender of life is nothing to sinking down into acknowledgement of inferiority.

John C. Calhoun

926. We know what we are, but know not what we may be.

William Shakespeare

927. Fortune knocks at every man's door once in a lifetime, but in a good many cases the man is in a neighboring saloon and does not hear her.

Mark Twain

928. Little things affect little minds.

Benjamin Disraeli

929. A law of nature rules that energy cannot be destroyed. You change it from coal to steam, from steam to power in turbines, but you do not destroy energy. In the same way, another law governs human activity and rules that honest effort cannot be lost, but that some day the proper benefits will be forthcoming.

Peter Speicher

930. Patience, and the mulberry leaf becomes a silk gown.

Chinese proverb

931. When there is no apparent reason for something happening, look for the financial gain

Anon.

Wise Words

932. **W**e triumph without glory when we conquer without danger.

Corneille

933. **W**hat is defeat? Nothing but education, nothing but the first step to something better.

Wendel Phillips

934. **I**f I were to prescribe one process in the training of men which is fundamental to success in any direction, it would be thorough-going training in the habit of accurate observation. It is a habit which every one of us should be seeking ever more to perfect.

Eugene G. Grace

935. **W**e have forty million reasons for failure, but not a single excuse.

Rudyard Kipling

936. **M**an is still responsible. He must turn the alloy of modern experience into the steel of mastery and character. His success lies not with the starts, but with himself. He must carry on the fight of self-correction and discipline. He must fight mediocrity as sin.

Frank. C. Williams

937. **T**he surest way to corrupt a youth is to instruct him to hold in higher esteem those who think alike than those who think differently.

Friedrich Nietzsche

Wise Words

938. Regret is an appalling waste of energy; you can't build on it; it's only good for wallowing in.
Katherine Mansfield

939. Work is the greatest thing in the world, so we should always save some of it for tomorrow.
Don Herold

940. The waste of life occasioned by trying to do too many things at once is appalling.
Orison S. Marden

941. Never hire someone who knows less than you do about what he's been hired to do.
Malcomb S. Forbes

942. The policy of being too cautious is the greatest risk of all.

Jawaharial Nehru

943. The real difference between men is energy. A strong will, a settled purpose, an invincible determination can accomplish almost anything; and in this lies the distinction between great men and little men.
Thomas Fuller

944. If at first you don't succeed, you'll get a lot of advice.

Anon.

945. Even if you're on the right track, you'll get run over if you just sit there.
Arthur Godfrey

Wise Words

946. The only people who never fail are those who never try.

Ilka Chase

947. What has puzzled us before seems less mysterious, and the crooked paths look straighter as we approach the end.

Jean Paul Richter

948. No gain is so certain as that which proceeds from the economical use of what you already have.

Latin proverb

949. An error doesn't become a mistake until you refuse to correct it.

Orlando Battista

950. He who thinks he can afford to be negligent is not far from being poor.

Samuel Johnson

951. A concept is stronger than a fact.

Charlotte P. Gillman

952. Sometimes one pays most for the things one gets for nothing.

Albert Einstein

953. The man who gets the most satisfactory results is not always

Wise Words

the man with the most brilliant single mind, but rather the man who can best coordinate the brains and talents of his associates.

W. Alton Jones

954.   We acquire the strengths we have overcome.

Ralph Waldo Emerson

955.   Imagination is our strongest tool – basically, the ability to see ordinary things in new ways.

Keith Herrmann

956.   Great intellects are skeptical.

Anon.

957.   The gent who wakes up and finds himself a success hasn't been asleep.

Wilson Mizner

958.   When a man has no reason to trust himself, he trusts to luck.

Ed Howe

959.   A single idea, if it is right, saves us an infinity of experiences.

Jacques Maritain

960.   All great discoveries are made by men whose feelings run ahead of their thinking.

Charles H. Parkhurst

Wise Words

961. The worst bankrupt in the world is the man who has lost his enthusiasm.
H.W. Arnold

962. A weak mind is like a microscope which magnifies trifling things but cannot receive great ones.
Lord Chesterfield

963. How many feasible projects have miscarried through despondence, strangled in their birth by a cowardly imagination.
Jeremy Collier

964. Creation is a drug I can't do without.
Cecil B. DeMille

965. Man is not imprisoned by habit. Great changes in him can be wrought by crisis once that crisis can be recognized and understood.
Norman Cousins

966. Some of us are like wheelbarrows…only useful when pushed, and very easily upset.
Jack Herbert

967. Entrepreneurs have more energy than most organizations can tolerate.
Anon.

968. Experience shows that success is due less to ability than to zeal. The winner is he who gives himself to his work, body and soul.
Charles Buxton

Wise Words

969. The way to be nothing is to do nothing.

Nathaniel Howe

970. Ignorance breeds monsters to fill up the vacancies of the world that are unoccupied by the verities of knowledge.

Horace Mann

971. Of all creatures on earth, we humans have the highest level of stupidity.

Cullen Hightower

972. Where we cannot invent, we may at least improve.

Charles C. Colton

973. Instinct is untaught ability.

Alexander Bain

974. We judge ourselves by what we feel capable of doing; others judge us by what we have done.

Longfellow

975. Good resolutions are simple checks that men draw on a bank where they have no account.

Oscar Wilde

976. Some people do first, think afterward, and then repent forever.

Thomas Secker

Wise Words

977. Poverty often deprives a man of all spirit and virtue. It is hard for an empty bag to stand upright.
Benjamin Franklin

978. Don't make excuses, make good.
Elbert Hubbard

979. You cannot depend on your eyes when your imagination is out of focus.
Mark Twain

980. That so few dare to be eccentric marks the chief danger of the time.
John Stuart Mill

981. The man is idle who can do something better.
Ralph Waldo Emerson

982. The least movement is of importance to all nature. The entire ocean is affected by a pebble.
Blaise Pascal

983. One cool judgement is worth a thousand hasty councils. The thing to do is to supply light, not heat.
Woodrow Wilson

984. The wisest mind has something yet to learn.
George Santayana

Wise Words

985. The only limit to realizing tomorrow is our doubts of today.
Franklin D. Roosevelt

986. The reward of the spirit who tries is the exercise not the goal.
E.V. Cooke

987. There are two times in a man's life when he should not speculate; when he can't afford it, and when he can.
Mark Twain

988. Half the word is composed of people who have something to say and can't, and the other half have nothing to say and keep on saying it.
Robert Frost

989. Before you try to become a better person, be the best person you know how to be now.
Anon.

990. If you aren't fired with enthusiasm, you'll be fired with enthusiasm.
Vince Lombardi

991. He who has a thing to sell and goes and whispers in a well is not as apt to get the dollars as he who climbs a tree and hollers.
Anon.

992. No man would listen to you talk if he didn't know he was next.
Ed Howe

Wise Words

993. **W**hat we call evil is simply ignorance bumping its head in the dark.

Henry Ford

994. **W**hen a fellow says, "It ain't the money but the principle of the thing," it's the money.

Frank McKinney "Kin" Hubbard

995. **T**o the timid and hesitating, everything is impossible because it seems so.

Walter Scott

996. **F**ind a purpose in life so big that it will challenge your every capacity to be your best.

David O. McKay

997. **N**ever be afraid to try something new.

Anon.

998. **D**on't be misled into believing that somehow the world owes you a living. The boy who believes that his parents, or the government, or anyone else owes him his livelihood and that he can collect it without labor will wake up one day and find himself working for another boy who did not have that belief and, therefore, earned the right to have others work for him.

David Sarnoff

999. **T**he artist who aims at perfection in everything achieves it in nothing.

Delacroix

Wise Words

1000. Before you try to make more of your life, make the most of what life has already given you.

Anon.

1001. Of all the sad words of tongue or pen, the saddest are these: "It might have been!"

John Greenleaf Whittier

Wise Words

Index

A

Abrashoff, Mike, 395
Adams, Henry Brooks, 778
Adams, John Quincy, 921
Adams, Scott, 199
Addison, Joseph, 847
Adizes, Ichak, 549
Ackerman, Bob, 486
Aeschylus, 615
African proverb, 507
Alain, 924
Alda, Alan, 761
Alderson, M.H., 500
Ali, Muhammad, 416, 561
Allen, David, 42
Allen, Woody, 63
Arabian proverb, 482
Archibald, R.C., 159
Aristotle, 818
Arkin, Alan, 66
Arnold, H.W., 961
Arnold, Wallace, 45
Ash, Mary Kay, 483
Assisi, St. Francis of, 678

Wise Words

B

Bacall, Lauren, 277
Bach, Richard, 233
Bacon, Francis, 626, 902
Baez, Joan, 251
Bailey, Gamaliel, 336
Bain, Alexander, 973
Baker, Roland C., 1
Ball, Ivern, 391, 608
Barad, Jill Elikann, 122
Barnes, Theodore W., 636
Barnum, P.T., 185, 722
Barron, C. W., 86
Barrie, J.M., 62
Barth, Joseph, 268
Batista, Randas Jose Vilela, 191
Battista, Orlando, 949
Baxter, Cecil, 273, 423
Bayol, Ben, 497
Beecher, Henry Ward, 649, 719
Beecher, John, 149
Belgian proverb, 487
Bell, Alexander Graham, 73
Bellamy, Guy, 653
Benet, Stephen Vincent, 481
Bennett, Arnold, 267
Bennette, Leslie, 563
Berenson, Bernard, 543
Berlin, Irving, 58
Berloiz, Hector, 123, 786
Bernard, Chester, 579

Wise Words

Berra, Yogi, 231
Bilbey, Sir Water, 346
Billings, Josh, 620, 643, 657, 785, 865
Birdseye, Clarence, 20
Blessington, Lady Marguerite, 98
Bolton, Robert, 602
Bonaparte, Napoleon, 96, 135, 333, 384, 433, 517, 897, 923
Bottome, Phyllis, 811
Bovee, Christian N., 812, 901
Bradbury, Ray, 347
Bradley, Bill, 407
Bradley, Omar M., 221, 498
Bradstreet, Anne, 150
Brault, Robert, 464
Brecht, Bertolt, 363
Brisban, Arthur, 624, 849
Brombeck, Erma, 472
Bronte, Emily, 418
Brown, William D., 161
Brower, Charles, 508
Browne, Merry, 310
Browning, Robert, 121, 272, 903
Bryan, William Jennings, 699
Bryant, Bear, 748
Buck, Pearl S., 242, 744
Buffett, Warren, 241, 380
Bulwer-Lytton, E.G., 900
Burnett, Leo, 511
Butler, Samuel, 522
Buxton, Charles, 968

Wise Words

C

Cage, John, 596
Calhoun, John C., 925
Calwell, Arthur, 537
Campbell, David, 676
Camus, Albert, 214, 645
Canetti, Elias, 890
Cannon, Damien, 590
Carlyle, Thomas, 69, 82, 895, 907
Carnegie, Andrew, 94, 912
Carnegie, Dale, 13, 129, 805
Carr, E. H., 219
Carty, Margaret, 714
Carver, George Washington, 772
Cary, Joyce, 41
Case, Mary, 574
Casson, Herbert N., 264, 892
Cato, 621
Chadwick, Hal, 669
Chalmers, Alan K., 854
Chase, Ilka, 946
Chazin, Susanne, 556, 651, 800
Chester, Henry, 266
Chesterfield, Lord, 205, 962
Chesterton, G.K., 536, 821
Chiang Kai-shek, Mme, 229
Chinese proverb, 53, 844, 930
Christie, Agatha, 409
Churchill, Winston, 11, 317, 646, 743
Cicero, 710
Clark, Joe, 662

Wise Words

Clarke, Arthur C., 684
Cleek, John, 585
Coblitz, David B., 328
Cohan, George M. 897
Cole, Edwin Louis, 731
Collier, Jeremy, 516, 963
Collier, Robert, 826
Collins, John, 115
Colton, Charles C., 728, 972
Conant, James B. 598
Confucius, 7, 732
Congreve, William, 910
Conrad, Joseph, 238
Cooke, E.V., 986
Coolidge, Calvin, 203
Corneille, 932
Costner, Kevin, 104
Cousins, Norman, 965
Coward, Noel, 38
Cowper, William, 915
Cox, Coleman, 261, 591
Curtis, Cyrus H., 909
Cumberland, Richard, 891

D

D'Angelo, Anthony J., 827
Dansen, H.E., 258
Darwin, Charles, 545
Davenant, William 866
Davis, Geena, 461
da Vinci, Leonardo, 308

Wise Words

Day, Clarence, 197
Dean, Dizzy, 428
Dean, Jimmy, 552
De Bono, Edward, 217
De Gaulle, Charles, 457
De Kooning, William, 230
Delacroix, 999
de La Rochefouchauld, Francois, 687
DeMille, Cecil B., 964
Deming, W. Edwards, 832
Demosthenes, 601
de Saint-Exupery, Antoine, 814
de Sales, St. Francis, 71
Descartes, Rene, 627
Devlin, Bernadette, 828
De Voto, Bernard, 862
Dexter, Bruce B., 721
Didion, Joan, 327
Disney, Walt, 829
Disraeli, Benjamin, 99, 524, 742, 859, 928
Ditka, Mike, 321
Doble, J. Frank, 572
Dowd, Maureen, 56
Drayton, William, 477
Drucker, Peter F., 130, 236, 470, 830
Dryden, John, 564, 659
Dunne, Finley P., 400
Dunsany, Lord, 918
Durant, Will, 438
Dutch proverb, 906
Dylan, Bob, 490

Wise Words

E

Earhart, Amelia, 125
Eastwood, Clint, 281
Eddings, David, 224
Edelston, Marty, 406, 539
Edison, Thomas A., 51, 256, 320, 468, 559, 717, 754, 852, 913
Edward, Tyron, 716
Einstein, Albert, 116, 269, 542, 703, 952
Eisner, Michael D., 243
Eisenhower, Dwight D., 677, 843
Ellington, Duke, 171
Ellison, Ralph, 831
Emerson, George B., 584
Emerson, Ralph Waldo, 95, 111, 176, 184, 290, 446, 501, 567, 606, 734, 834, 851, 858, 877, 917, 954, 981
Emmett, Rita, 97
English proverb, 289, 611, 813
English, Tomas D., 683
Epictitus, 128, 460, 632
Epicures, 215
Epworth, Jeremy C., 169
Erskine, Lord, 860
Etienne, Jean-Louis, 368
Euripides, 688
Ewing, Sam, 388

F

Farrell, Michael Kevin, 43
Faulkner, William, 885
Feather, William, 4, 582, 752
Fields, Debbie, 89

Wise Words

Fielding, Henry, 698
Fields, W.C., 691, 823
Fitzgerald, F. Scott, 413
Flood, Stephen, 225
Flynn, John Peter, 737
Forbes, Malcomb S., 146, 190, 351, 787, 941
Forbes, B.C., 701, 863
Ford, Henry, 226, 252, 284, 398, 541, 607, 700, 833, 993
Fortgang, Laura Berman, 133
Fosdick, Henry Emerson, 361
Foste, John W., 822
France, Anatole, 174, 323, 871
Francis, Clarence, 741
Frankfurter, Felix, 867
Franklin, Benjamin, 29, 192, 454, 753, 792, 894, 977
Freedman, Lewis, 789
French proverb, 367
Freud, Anna, 441
Frost, Robert, 988
Frostburg, Philip 548, 635, 749, 781
Fuller, Thomas, 943

G
Gandhi, Indira, 739
Gandhi, Mohandas K., 444, 523, 775
Garfield, James, 879
Geer, Carolyn T., 562
George, David Lloyd, 791, 880
George, William Lloyd, 442
Gerard, 259
German proverb, 313

Wise Words

Getty, J. Paul, 166
Giamatti, A. Bartlett, 403
Gibron, Kahlil, 196
Gibson, Althea, 276
Gide, Andre, 22
Gillman, Charlotte P., 951
Giovanni, Nikki, 270
Glasgow, Arnold H., 756
Glasgow, Ellen, 802
Glenn, John, 664
Goddard, Robert H., 730
Godfrey, Arthur, 945
Goethe, 105, 341, 492, 547, 782, 887
Goldberg, Natalie, 147
Goldsmith, Oliver, 809
Goldstein, Stanley, 322
Goldwyn, Sam, 255
Golisano, Tom, 614
Goodwin, Jim, 90
Grace, William G., 934
Graham, Billy, 372
Granatelli, Andy, 526
Greeley, Horace, 806
Green, Harold, 353
Grey, Zane, 587
Grimes, Martha, 316
Grisolia, Philip A., 25, 172, 187, 206, 565, 689

H

Hailsham, Lord, 514
Half, Robert, 3, 40, 88, 228, 293, 445, 496, 644

Wise Words

Hannibal, 580
Hansberry, Lorraine, 314
Hardy, Thomas, 155
Harrell, Wilson L., 234
Harriman, Edward H., 905
Harris, Sidney J., 287
Hart, Gary, 17
Haskins, Henry S., 420, 530
Hawkes, Dean, 804
Hayes, John, R., 427
Hazlett, Thomas W., 213
Hazlitt, William, 325, 484, 720, 872
Hebrew proverb, 760
Hedges, Joe E., 884
Hemingway, Ernest, 824
Henrichs, Garth, 360
Herbert, Jack, 966
Herford, Oliver, 776
Herold, Don, 119, 939
Herrmann, Keith, 955
Hesburgh, Theodore, 52, 432
Heyde, Mary Ellen, 250
Hightower, Cullen, 245, 971
Hill, Napoleon, 107
Hilton, Conrad, 44
Hind, James F., 356
Hodgson, Ralph, 673
Hoffer, Eric, 883
Holm, Celeste, 348
Holmes, Sr., Oliver Wendell, 349
Holtz, Lou, 837
Honda, Soichiro, 210

Wise Words

Hopf, H.A., 727
Hoover, Herbert, 354
Horace, 702, 842
Howard, Ron, 117
Howard, Sidney, 439
Howe, Ed, 794, 920, 958, 992
Howe, Nathaniel, 969
Hubbard, Elbert, 77, 145, 175, 335, 978
Hubbard, Kin, 471, 994
Hubbell, Carl, 329
Hugo, Victor, 5, 76, 696, 899
Huneker, James G., 715
Hunt, Diana S., 660
Hutchins, Robert M., 735
Huxley, Aldous, 28, 131, 532
Huxley, Thomas, 551

I

Iacocca, Lee, 513, 768
Inge, William, 138, 202
Ingersoll, Robert G., 435
Inman, R., 751
Irving, Washington, 459, 592
Ivins, Molly, 426

J

Jacks, L.P., 151
Jackson, Andrew, 736
James, Carla B., 546
James, William, 443, 767, 889
Japanese proverb, 296

Wise Words

Jarvik, Dr. Robert, 6
Jay, John C., 515
Jefferson, Thomas, 30, 402
Jenkins, J., 613
Johnson, Kimberly, 473
Johnson, Michael, 118, 198
Johnson, Stewart B., 12
Johnson, Samuel, 78, 216, 553, 697, 950
Jones, Alice Ward., 919
Jones, Franklin P., 67, 667
Jones, W. Alton, 953
Jong, Erica, 144, 495
Jordan, David S., 455
Joubert, Joseph, 869

K

Kahn, Philippe, 625
Kaiser, Henry, J., 639
Karolyi, Bela, 777
Katayama, Nihachiro, 581, 594
Katz, Ellie, 529
Kaunda, Kenneth, 502
Keller, Helen, 275, 378
Kelley, David M., 189
Keillor, Garrison, 301
Kemp, Jack, 780
Kennedy, John F., 19
Kenny, Elizabeth, 450
Kettering, Charles, 467, 694
Keyes, Jr., Ken S., 294
Kiechel III, Walter, 324

Wise Words

King, Jr., Martin Luther, 164
Kingley, Charles, 369
Kipling, Rudyard, 935
Kissinger, Henry A. 300
Klemme, E.J., 893
Knight, Bobby, 304
Knight, Philip N., 648
Knudsen, William S., 568, 597
Koestler, Arthur, 342, 661
Krause, Karl, 593
Kroc, Ray, 160, 518
Kroll, Alex, 630
Kwolek, Stephanie, 188

L

L'Amour, Louis, 54, 452
Land, Edwin H. 386
Landers, Ann, 178
Landon, Michael, 49
Lardner, Ring, 815
Larson, Doug, 311, 396, 544, 612
Latham, Peter, 421
Latin proverb, 948
Laughlin, Owen, 109, 383
Lauren, Ralph, 422
Law, Vernon, 586
Lee, Harper, 36
Lerner, Max, 616
Lessing, Doris, 712
Letterman, Elmer, 705
Levinson, Sam, 784

Wise Words

Lewin, Kurt, 389
Lippmann, Walter, 729
Lincoln, Abraham, 18, 377, 449, 479
Lindbergh, Anne Morrow, 671
Ling, James, 183
Ling, Nicholas, 656
Link, Henry C., 733
Lombardi, Vince, 9, 153, 271, 570, 990
London, Jack, 799
Longfellow, 180, 604, 898, 974
Lord, Shirley, 475
Lucado, Max, 195
Lukas, Wayne, 68
Lynn, Loretta, 50
Lyon, Mary, 350

M
MacLeish, Archibald, 540, 724
Mann, Horace, 103, 970
Mansfield, Katherine, 938
Marden, Orison S., 940
Maritain, Jacques, 959
Mark 9:23, 265
Marquis, Don., 201
Marx, Karl, 856
Mason, Andrew V., 156
Massinger, Philip, 375
Mattingly, Don, 528
Maugham, Somerset, 126, 371
Maynard, Robertine, 436
Maxwell, William, 249

Wise Words

McArthur, Douglas, 373
McArthur, Peter, 57
McKay, David O., 996
McMurtry, Larry, 283, 412
Meltzer, Bernard, 583
Miline, A.A., 246
Mill, John Stewart, 170, 535, 980
Miller, Henry, 79
Mitchell, Donald G., 779
Mizner, Wilson, 738, 957
Montesquieu, 408
Monod, Adolph, 668
Moore, Troy, 674
Morgan, Arthur E., 431
Morgan, J.P., 208
Morley, Christopher, 47, 686, 861
Morris, Ken, 291
Muhammad, 795
Muir, John, 619

N
Nash, Edward, 533, 759
Nash, Ogden, 839
Nehru, Jawaharial, 690, 942
Newhart, Bob, 521
Niblack, Griff, 343
Nicklaus, Jack, 345
Nietzsche, Friedrich, 299, 633, 788, 836, 937
Norris, Kathleen, 302

O

Wise Words

O'Casey, Sean, 766
O'Connor, Sandra Day, 48
Ogilvie, Lloyd John, 796
Onassis, Aristotle, 617
Orben's Current Comedy, 746
Orwell, George, 825
Osgood, Charles, 152
Outlaw, Frank, 16

P
Parker, Christopher, 235
Parkhurst, Charles H., 960
Parkinson, C. Northcote, 771
Pascal, Blaise, 982
Paterno, Joe, 307
Patton, Jr., George S., 31, 120, 465, 707
Paul, Swraj, 274
Pavlova, Anna, 374
Peale, Norman Vincent, 555
Peck, M. Scott, 60,
Penner, Pansy, 723
Penzias, Arno, 773
Pepper, Claude, 478
Peterman, John, 193, 429, 510
Peterson, Wilfred, 263
Petit-Senn, J., 911
Philipotts, Eden, 874
Phillips, Frederick, 397
Phillips, Wendel, 385, 933
Picasso, Pablo, 693
Pickford, Mary, 709

Wise Words

Pickins, T. Boone, 339
Pitt, Alan Ashley, 85
Pitt, William, 878
Plato, 207
Plautus, 488, 875
Poe, Edgar Allan, 864
Powell, Colin, 34, 257
Prather, Hugh, 681
Price, Reynolds, 309
Prochnow, Herbert V., 637
Prothro, Tommy, 337
Proust, Marcel, 448, 816
Proverb, 810, 855
Proverbs 29:18, 419
Purcell, Corky, 143

Q

R

Rand, Ayn, 493, 764
Rashad, Phylicia, 200
Raspberry, William, 148
Redmond, William A., 344
Redstone, Sumner, 382
Reed, John, 763
Reichmann, Paul, 622
Richter, Jean Paul, 947
Rickenbacker, Edward, 634
Ringgold, Faith, 33
Robbins, Tom, 220
Roberts, Kevin, 61

Wise Words

Robinson, Sugar Ray, 480
Roche, Boyle, 888
Rockefeller, Jr., John, D., 359, 603,
Rockne, Knute, 726
Rogers, Will, 139, 232, 853
Rohatyn, Felix, 295
Roloff, Becky, 127
Rommel, 237
Rooney, Mickey, 27
Roosevelt, Franklin D., 758, 840, 985
Roosevelt, Theodore, 8, 80, 338, 558
Roux, Joseph, 209
Ruskin, John, 218
Russell, Bertrand, 39, 91, 411, 695
Rutherford, Lord, 525
Ryan, Jim, 247

S

Sadat, Anwar, 212
Sallust, 881
Salk, Jonas, 364
Santayana, George, 984
Sarnoff, David, 21, 998
Schmidt, Helmut, 838
Schneider, Diana, 312
Schopenhauer, Arthur, 136
Schrempp, Juergen, 765
Schwab, Charles M., 244, 850
Schwartz, Tony, 410
Schweitzer, Albert, 132
Scott, Walter, 882, 995

Wise Words

Seaton, George, 755
Secker, Thomas, 976
Seinfeld, Jerry, 466
Seneca, 916
Setani, Joaquin, 108
Shaffer, Robert H., 32
Shakespeare, William, 650, 926
Shanahan, Eileen, 654
Shaw, George Bernard, 162, 248, 414, 629, 870
Shedd, John A., 110
Sills, Beverly, 575
Silzer, Parker W., 641
Simborg, Philip 352
Sirkin, Spring, 424
Slim, W.J., 578
Smiles, Samuel, 873
Smith, June, 666
Smith, Logan P., 334
Socrates, 896
Sons, Ray, 569
Sowell, Thomas, 451
Spanish proverb, 114
Speicher, Peter, 929
Spock, Benjamin, 279
Spurgeon, Charles, 573
Stein, Howard, 75
Stengel, Casey, 453
Stephens, James, 280
Stern, Judith, 876
Storey, 819
Stevenson, Adlai, 142
Strode, Muriel, 83

Wise Words

Suzuki, Shunyu, 362
Sweetland, Ben, 285
Swid, Stephen, 394
Swift, Jonathan, 588
Switzer, Maurice, 682
Syrus, Publilius, 102
Szent-Gyorgyi, Albert, 405

T
Tagore, Rabindranath, 708
Talmud, The, 100
Taylor, Elizabeth, 841
Taylor, Glen, 610
Tennyson, Alfred Lord, 165
Tharp, Twyla, 240
Thatcher, Margaret, 10, 106, 366
Thomas, Danny, 845
Thoreau, Henry David, 26, 72, 158, 506, 599, 638, 706, 808
Thornton, Donald, 113
Todd, Mike, 494
Tomlin, Lily, 393
Toynby, Arnold, 286,
Tremeer, Henri, 154
Truman, Harry S., 87, 239, 745
Trump, Donald, 489
Twain, Mark, 124, 134, 211, 292, 370, 440, 531, 665, 803, 868, 927, 987
Tyger, Frank, 93, 167, 672

U

Wise Words

V

Van Buren, Martin, 846
Van Gogh, Vincent, 447
Valmy, Christine, 298
Van Horne, William, 315
Veeck, Bill, 713
Vincent, John H., 157
Vizinczey, Stephen, 37
Voltaire, 84, 318, 390, 401
Von Bismark, Otto, 503
von Braun, Wernher, 179, 505
von Clausewitz, Karl, 415
von Savant, Marilyn, 519

W

Waitley, Dennis, 140, 204
Waldrip, Mary H., 458
Walton, Sam, 357
Ward, William A., 305, 463, 557, 680
Warhol, Andy, 24
Watson, Sr., Thomas J., 456
Webster, Daniel, 254
Weinbaum, Dave, 15, 59, 141, 222, 332
Wells, Charles, 848
West, Mae, 177
White, Steward E., 914
Whittier, John Greenleaf, 1001
Wilde, Oscar, 70, 227, 550, 975
Wilder, Billy, 65
Williams, Ben, 297, 365, 798
Williams, Christopher, 14

Wise Words

Williams, Frank C., 936
Williams, Tennessee, 182
Wilson, Woodrow, 476, 571, 750, 983
Winfrey, Oprah, 331
Winston, Clara, 355
Winters, Jonathan, 319
Wittgenstein, Ludwig, 437
Wolff, Tobias, 379
Wooden, John, 538, 675
Wylie, Philip, 303

X

Y
Young, Eva, 576

Z

Anon. 2, 23, 35, 46, 55, 64, 74, 81, 92, 101, 112, 137, 163, 168, 173, 181, 186, 194, 223, 253, 262, 278, 282, 288, 306, 326, 330, 340, 358, 376, 381, 387, 392, 399, 404, 417, 425, 430, 434, 462, 469, 474, 485, 491, 499, 504, 509, 520, 527, 534, 554, 560, 566, 577, 589, 595, 600, 605, 609, 618, 623, 628, 631, 640, 642, 647, 652, 655, 658, 663, 670, 679, 685, 692, 704, 711, 718, 725, 740, 747, 757, 762, 769, 770, 774, 783, 790, 793, 797, 801, 807, 817, 820, 835, 857, 886, 904, 908, 922. 931, 944, 956, 967, 989, 991, 997, 1000

Wise Words

**For your convenience, you may
write the numbers of your favorite truths on these two pages.**

Wise Words

To order additional copies of this book, please see page 158.

Wise Words

To order additional copies of

WISE WORDS

1001 Truths to Inspire, Enlighten and Enrich Everyday Life

❑ Complete this Order Form. ❑ Attach it to your check in the appropriate amount made payable to Wise Words. ❑ Mail the Order Form and Check to:

Wise Words, POB 368, Huntley IL 60142-0368

Please **PRINT CLEARLY** the following information: QUANTITY ❑

Your Name _____

Mailing Address _____

City / State / Zip _____

Email Address▲ _____

▲ **NOTE:** Because we value your privacy as much as you do, we do not share any customer information with anyone.

Shipping & Handing Options Within the U.S. and Territories (1)

Your Options	Book Price	Estimated Delivery *	Type of Mail Service	Shipping/ Handling	TOTAL COST, USD
1	$24.95	1 to 3 Days	Priority Mail	$6.50	$31.25
2	$24.95	3 to 5 Days	First Class	$5.65	$30.60
3	$24.95	5 to 7 Days	Parcel Post	$5.35	$30.30
4	$24.95	6 to 8 Days	Media Mail	$4.95	$29.90

*Estimated Delivery Days shown are approximate and do not include day of receipt by USPS.

(1) For costs and estimated deliver times to Canada and elsewhere, email Staff@PhilGrisolia.com

www.ingramcontent.com/pod-product-compliance
Lightning Source LLC
Chambersburg PA
CBHW071435160426
43195CB00013B/1904